Global Impact

Award Winning Performance Programs
from Around the World

Sylvia B. Odenwald
and
William G. Matheny

IRWIN
Professional Publishing®
Chicago • London • Singapore

◥◤ **Times Mirror**
Ⓜ **Higher Education Group**

Library of Congress Cataloging-in-Publication Data

Odenwald, Sylvia.
   Global impact : award winning performance programs from around the world / Sylvia B. Odenwald, William G. Matheny.
      p. cm.
   Includes index.
   ISBN 0–7863–0958–X
   1. Total quality management—Case studies. 2. Industrial management—Case studies. I. Matheny, William G. (William Gene), 1945–   .
   HD62.15.033   1996
   658.5′62—dc20   96–6441

Printed in the United States of America
1 2 3 4 5 6 7 8 9 0 BP 3 2 1 0 9 8 7 6

Contents

Introduction

Corporate executives and managers struggle daily with the increased pace and complexity of the global business world. Mark Youngblood provocatively describes the enormity of change in his book, *Eating the Chocolate Elephant* (Micrografix, 1994). He suggests:

> Imagine a chocolate elephant. Four thousand pounds of solid chocolate—ten feet high at the shoulder, fifteen feet long, eight feet across—and it is your job to eat it. The idea of eating a chocolate elephant is so monumentally staggering that it is hard to know where or how to start.

This situation can be a problem even for chocoholics. Similarly, the changes in the world today are so staggering that it is difficult to know how to deal with them or even where to begin.

Yes, today's global marketplace is characterized by upheaval and transformation. This is an era in which information is communicated and work is conducted across borders, cultures, companies, industries, locations, and functions with new emerging demands on workers and companies around the world. And these changes are occurring faster than the speed of sound—breaking not just barriers of speed but the realms of cyberspace.

We are so bombarded with our launch into the 21st century that it is extremely difficult to find opportunity in the chaos. We are so busy echoing our frustrations with the challenges transnational companies face that we too often overlook the progressive strides in the area of performance. The purpose of this book is to focus on the positive, results-oriented programs being implemented today.

American companies are often seen as trendsetters in performance and training. While corporations from other countries research and benchmark U.S. best practices, the excellent work of organizations in other areas of the world is usually ignored or hidden—as in Southeast Asia where companies are hesitant to share their training programs since they consider effective training their competitive edge over other corporations in their industry.

Book Focus

As multinationals enter new markets seeking customers and employees whose cultures and ways of conducting business are often quite different, they need to understand what business issues are important in those countries. This book presents case studies of some of the best human resource performance and management processes from the main regions of the world: The Americas, Europe, the Middle East and Africa, and the Pacific Rim. The company examples are presented by corporate training specialists and consultants who were actively involved in the process. An explanation of procedures along with the impact of the results from the programs are discussed. Although it is not possible to select programs from every country, industry, and performance area, a variety is presented as well as a few case studies from government agencies and nonprofit organizations. Major topic areas are listed in Figure 1, and Figure 2 provides an industry list. The regions covered and the companies discussed within each region are outlined in Figure 3.

Figure 1

Program Topics

Specific topic areas include the following:

- Redesigning corporate culture.
- Mutual gains training—a collaborative approach to union/management relations.
- Restructuring and downsizing.
- Competency assessment and training redesign.
- Participatory management.
- Setting up a corporate university.
- Executive development.
- Changing the HR/Training role.
- Personnel development.
- Developing individualized, open learning modules.
- Environmental protection training.
- Productivity improvement.
- Management development.
- Designing a training system.
- Supervisory training.
- International training.

Figure 2
Industries

Types of industries targeted:
- Pharmaceutical
- Electronics
- Automobile
- Health care
- Energy supplier
- Agricultural agency
- Computers
- Multinational conglomerate
- Post office
- Banking
- Airplane parts suppliers
- Roads department
- Telecommunications
- Manufacturing
- Iron and steel
- Lighting fixtures
- Utility
- Cosmetics
- Insurance
- Coal mining
- Oil and gas
- Trade company
- Cleaning service

Figure 3
Organizations by Country

THE AMERICAS:

Canada
Glaxo Wellcome Inc.
Canada Post Corporation
SaskPower
Ontario Hydro

United States of America
Motorola
Praxair Surface Technologies
SmithKline Beecham

Central America
Instituto Interamericano de Cooperación
   para la Agricultura

South America
Amil
Unibanco
Avon

EUROPE:

Western Europe
Personnel Development - at Draegerwerke
AG, Volksbank, GMAC, and Dresdner
Bank

Scotland
Standard Life Assurance Company
Motorola Cellular Subscribe Group

Scandinavia
ISS
Louis Poulsen

Novo Nordisk
East Asiatic Company
Telia

Central and Eastern Europe
Radisson Hotels International

MIDDLE EAST AND AFRICA:

Israel
Teva Pharmaceutical Industries Ltd.

South Africa
The Free State Roads Department
Richards Bay Coal Terminal
Iron and Steel Corporation

PACIFIC RIM:

China
Motorola (China) Electronics Ltd.

Korea
Samsung

Southeast Asia
Management Training - Malaysia

Japan
Nippon Telegraph and Telephone
Mitsubishi Electric
Sanwa Bank
Texas Instruments Japan
NEC Corp.
Omron Corporation

Current Issues and Future Trends

Global Impact expands the earlier research and information presented in *Global Training: How to Design a Program for the Multinational Corporation* and *Global Solutions for Teams: Moving from Collision to Collaboration.* As a background for the case studies, each chapter begins with a review of current issues within the specific country or region. These issues directly affect and influence the training and performance within that geographic area. Although every country is not included in this research, the 14 chapters provide valuable data, case studies, and projected future performance trends in each region. The conclusion focuses on emerging trends that will drive personnel development during the next 10 years.

Worldwide Contributors

A special thanks to the experienced contributors who researched the current issues and future trends in the countries where they work: Asma Abdullah, Peter Beckschi, Maura Fallon, Beverly Forté, Wolf-Dieter Gebhardt, P.A. Grobler, Bob Harris, Joel Hastings, Tadashi Iwaki, Bob Kuchinsky, Françoise Morissette, John Mullin, Hugo Nisenbaum, Serge Ogranovitch, Kevin Reynolds, John Shuchmaker, Susan Vonsild, Gayle Watson, and David Weiss. They were all involved in the case studies and directly impacted the success of these programs. Without their expertise this book would not have been possible.

Selection of Case Studies

The case studies in *Global Impact* are examples of successful programs for the companies spotlighted. They are called award-winning rather than *best practices*. This is a conscious choice. What may be a best practice in one organization—if translated verbatim—may be totally wrong for another. The term *benchmarking* is similar. If a company benchmarks processes and performance from a competitor and transfers them to their workforce, they are already 5 to 10 years behind in implementation of the benchmarked corporation. Also the innovations may not be appropriate without major changes. Every company needs to study, observe, research, and benchmark ideas and processes—but only to spark creative ideas. Best practices and benchmarking are helpful if used mainly for brainstorming and obtaining innovative processes. Therefore, the case studies discussed in this book are to provide a frame of reference. This is the premise of the book and our wish for you as you read it.

Today many of tomorrow's mega-opportunities are just being conceived and born. Partnerships are being formed, competencies assembled, and experiments conducted. Those corporations with a view of where they want to go and who can assemble and orchestrate resources across the globe have a chance to capture the future. The opportunities of a new era are here for those companies who want to blaze new trails in the international arena.

REGION 1: THE AMERICAS

CHAPTER 1

Canada

David S. Weiss, Partner
Bob Harris, **Bob Kuchinsky**, and
Françoise Morissette, Senior Consultants
Geller, Shedletsky & Weiss

CURRENT ISSUES

A savvy chief executive officer of a major food manufacturer, when asked recently to account for his company's success, indicated that strategy is not as critical as once assumed. In his view, everyone in his industry sees things the same way, and he can fit a *tissue* between his company's strategy and the competition's. The only differences lie in how his company implements and adapts that strategy.

Canadian executives have moved past a focus on developing the perfect strategy. Attention is now focused on being adaptable in making a strategy work and managing change advantageously. This view has meant an altered definition of what kind of workforce is necessary and a different mandate for human resources. How this new expectation for human resources is being achieved in Canada is the focus of this chapter.

In the growth economy of the 1980s, the objective for human resource departments was to produce a continuous stream of able, well-trained employees to do the work that common wisdom and fixed precepts dictated had to be done. To attract the right people, companies needed also to maintain a position as being an employer of choice. In general, the main role of human resources was to focus on *work readiness assurance.*

Human resources did its work by ensuring that the right people were hired, trained, promoted, and groomed for senior positions, with mistakes taken care of through termination. The careful development of policies and procedures to ensure that people were able to perform in a consistent manner was a priority. The attractiveness of an employer was re-enforced by generous benefit plans and pension packages. The success of human resource departments was measured by how well they could attract and retain the *best* people to make the proven formulas for success work in their companies.

A Changing Business Climate

A change in the business climate has had a direct effect on human resources. Much less reliance is now placed on proven formulas for success, and much more reliance on building an adaptive culture. Effective human resource departments now position themselves differently within organizations with the intention of being part of that adaptive culture as well as supporting it.

The best-practice human resources initiatives that have emerged over the last few years are all aimed at creating that adaptive culture. The goal now is to develop tactics that will result in employees who have comfort with change, possess multiple competencies, and adapt to different kinds of customer expectations. These employees can handle the dramatic changes in organizations brought about by higher customer expectations, competition, information technology and process improvements, and downward pressure on costs.

Human resource departments that cannot find a mechanism to contribute to the adaptive culture find their position threatened within companies. Formerly, human resources was in the position of being a monopoly service provider within organizations, but there are currently a plethora of alternative service providers who compete for outsourced human resources work. These competitors to internal human resource services have been designed to excel in the administrative and tracking responsibilities found under the old *work readiness assurance* mandate.

Human resource departments that exhibit best practices today are finding a way to add value to an adaptive culture. They continue to be invited to join in the executive decision-making process. The head of the function usually reports directly to the president and is a peer player among the executive team in making major contributions to macro transformations in the company to align human potential to the strategic focus of the enterprise.

Creating the Adaptive Culture

In organizations where the human resource department has risen to the challenge of contributing to the adaptive culture, a decision is often made to outsource *the work readiness assurance* tasks and focus on human resources consulting and strategic management of the human asset base. Some of the strategies that are employed by those human resource departments include the following:

- Creating strategies to enable employees to experience themselves as empowered (rather than empowering people, which no one can do for another person).
- Creating job employability so people can always be employed versus treating job security as an entitlement.
- Transforming line management to leaders who are enabling others to create breakthroughs in adaptive cultures.
- Using information technology to reduce risk, human error, and hierarchy within organizations so senior executives can have access to necessary information directly.
- Removing *concurrent review approval processes* from the system requiring no more than two signatures on any document.
- Playing a major role in building trust and modeling value behaviors in the work environment.
- Creating alternative dispute resolution processes with managers and unions if they are operating within that organizational situation.
- Ensuring that changes within the organization are aligned so the *white space* between organizational functions does not limit the ability of the company to provide maximum customer satisfaction.

The role of human resources within Canadian companies in creating the adaptive culture is divided into three sections:

- *Creating culture change in the organization*
  This section focuses on a case study in which a human resource department championed a new set of values and behaviors within the entire company. By getting everyone involved, it was possible to integrate smoothly a company acquired recently for strategic purposes. Other examples of how human resource departments in Canada have contributed to culture change are also illustrated in this section.
- *Creating the adaptive culture through alternative dispute resolution processes*
  A union management situation is highlighted in which an entirely new method of working together was identified through mutual gains negotiating. Through this intervention, the organization has been more

effective. A peaceful coexistence between the management and the union has been achieved, which transformed a previously inflexible and adversarial situation. A full exploration of this process and how it can be achieved is explained by Dr. David Weiss in *Beyond the Walls of Conflict* (Irwin, 1996).

• *Creating the adaptive culture through transition with dignity*
Many organizations have decided to focus their human resource departments on the process of downsizing during this time of organizational change. This section discusses how a career transition center was set up in a major utility in Ontario to help them transform their organization and allow people to leave their enterprise with the maximum capability of finding another job and with their dignity intact.

All these case studies involved leadership within the companies and the consulting assistance of the human resources consulting firm of Geller, Shedletsky & Weiss. These organizational change stories are recounted here with the permission of representatives from each of these organizations.

Creating Culture Change in the Organization

The culture of an organization has a pervasive influence over how people do things, how they behave, and even how they think. Organizational culture can have two faces: it can be the healthy, adaptive means by which a company attains success, or it can become a barrier to success by paralyzing a company.

Culture changes slowly over time on an ongoing basis, but there are occasions when greater speed is needed for survival. At that point, the change in culture needs to be managed. Two companies—Glaxo Wellcome and Canada Post—faced with culture change have explored the challenges and describe their adaptive responses.

Glaxo Wellcome Inc.

In 1994, Glaxo decided it needed to reshape its strategic framework to correspond with business changes within the pharmaceutical industry. The company redefined its mission and vision and identified five key strategies to keep it on track. Flexible tactics that could adapt to circumstances would support these broad strategic intentions.

Based upon Glaxo Wellcome's vision—*to grow our business profitably by becoming a partner with our customers and the leader in the industry in improving disease outcomes in the health care system*—it was necessary to identify key strategies that would help the company be adaptive in fulfilling the vision.

The final choices looked at the company from different perspectives. When added together, they represent an integrated view of the business. The first theme was to become customer focused and develop behaviors within the culture that supported a customer orientation. Glaxo Wellcome is in a competitive industry, and the second theme was concerned with building into the company greater capability to design key processes that would make for a competitive advantage.

Not wanting to be strangled by practices that had once been successful but were no longer relevant, another key element was to free people to improve or eliminate other processes that had lived past their usefulness. Since markets shift and change, part of the strategy had to include a mechanism to help Glaxo Wellcome shift and change, so it could capitalize on the greatest opportunities for growth. Finally, Glaxo Wellcome estimated that building a strong positive culture was the necessary underpinning to achieve all of the other key elements.

Looking at the key culture element, an assumption was made that values create behaviors and behaviors shape the culture. Accordingly, great emphasis was placed upon having *living* corporate values. They could not just be words on posters to decorate the walls or on cards that employees could tuck into their desks. The values had to have intrinsic meaning to employees and had to be seen as worthwhile if they were to be adopted and honored.

Myles Harrigan, vice president of human resources within Glaxo Wellcome, was aware also that imposing values on people does not have a particularly good track record. Instead, a way had to be found that would allow the values to be an expression of what people thought and what was already important to them. The decision was to launch an initiative involving every employee of Glaxo Wellcome. Everyone would have input into the selection of values and in identifying behaviors that would support or clash with a given value.

The process was designed to be divided into five phases. Phase One consisted of management input and consolidation. During this phase, senior executives and managers were invited to participate in workshops where they selected the seven most important values for the company. The behaviors associated with these values were considered and what impact those values could have on them individually and on the company. They considered the impact of the values on productivity, profitability, morale, employee satisfaction, and other dimensions. They also estimated what it would take to make the values a reality, the barriers that might be encountered in implementing them, and the next steps to take.

The values selected had to represent an overlap between corporate and personal values. This requirement heightened the chances that the exercise would have individual meaning to employees and would be much more likely to be adopted as guiding principles for everyday behavior. A democratic process was used to select the final values.

The next phase involved employee input and consolidation of the values deeper into the organization. The objectives of this phase were as follows:
- To involve all employees.
- To address elements requiring change.
- To increase awareness of desirable behaviors, processes, and systems.
- To integrate with other key initiatives and establish benchmarks to measure progress.

A consolidation team of managers and front-line employees was formed from a cross-section of Glaxo Wellcome employees. Their role was to review the nominated values and behaviors for completeness and consistency, ensure that the choices were realistic, consolidate them into one meaningful set of values and behaviors, and develop a format for communication.

The third phase was to introduce action planning into normal working teams, which served as a good reality check. All too often, companies formally claim values that have little connection to the working reality of employees. To identify and examine any differences between the established informal values of the company and the proposed changes, team leaders led discussions of the values already present within each group. Then, a comparison was made with the nominated Glaxo Wellcome values and an analysis of gaps was completed. Each team identified desirable behaviors that would support the process, thought through how the process could be rolled out, and determined communication and training requirements.

Phase Four, which will be conducted in 1996, is implementation, where transformation, re-engineering, and other organizational processes and systems are aligned to the values. The final phase is a commitment to continuous improvement. Glaxo Wellcome believes that this process, built over the span of two years, has provided them with the corporate capabilities to create a new reality and a strong positive culture.

A sign of this changed reality was the smooth integration of a separate company, Wellcome, into the new Glaxo Wellcome, Inc., during this process. The Executive team chose to leverage the strengths of the participative values initiative as part of the integration exercise when Wellcome was acquired. The objective was to allow everyone to consider the values that would prevail in the new culture. The process encouraged an open dialogue for what the new organization would look like and how it would be for people to work in it.

A successful conclusion to the initiative allowed the new company to avoid a stage of misunderstanding that is typical of organizations that have changed shape through acquisition. It put the focus cleanly on integration and sent a consistent message to employees that their values, combined with corporate needs, do indeed live.

Canada Post Corporation

Canada Post underwent a change in status in 1982 from being a Federal Government Department to that of a Crown Corporation. Their new mandate was to generate profitable revenue and operate in a way to support that goal. Once virtually without competition, the face of Canada Post's business has been changed by fax, voice mail, e-mail, and customer-driven courier companies.

Since its change in status, Canada Post has worked hard at creating an adaptive culture. Extensive efforts were made to improve the efficiency of processes, modernize equipment, upgrade products, and multiply access points to customers. In 1994, under the leadership of newly appointed president Georges Clermont, Canada Post took one more step. It initiated a new phase in continuous improvement through a customer focus initiative.

This initiative was in response to surveys that revealed that the levels of service delivery, both for corporate and individual customers, would benefit from improvement. The challenge was to have that message reach the 54,000 employees of Canada Post, and have them create better, faster, friendlier service every working day.

This initiative arose from the broader change that Canada Post decided it would need to be successful in the next century. A key strategic decision was to create a Learning Institute, which would increase the ability of the organization and its employees to learn. Not a place fixed in physical space or time, the Learning Institute is the adaptive method by which human resource initiatives can be delivered across Canada.

"Over the past decade, the corporation has made huge investments in state-of-the-art technology. But it will be dead in ten years if its employees don't start to think like entrepreneurs rather than government employees." That statement by President Clermont clarified the value of the Learning Institute to the organization.

On a practical level, the Institute was backed by resources—a healthy budget that tripled the training fund per employee. Partnerships with Queen's University and the University of Montreal were formed to link the Institute to available research in management practice.

The Learning Institute has three areas of focus:
- Culture change.
- Job skills upgrading.
- The development of leadership and people management competencies.

The Learning Institute decided to achieve adaptability within Canada Post by equipping between 500 and 800 employees with the skills necessary to become part-time trainers. Employees are self-selected or nominated by others and go through a train-the-trainer program, which enables them to be a trainer for a maximum of 20 days a year. This decision creates a critical mass of change agents and a momentum for culture change, plus the bonus of giving employees a chance to expand their skills.

Phase One: Design

Canada Post began a Culture Change Customer Service Plus initiative. As part of the cascading tactics, a program that outlined the basic concepts of Service Plus was designed first for front-line employees. Next, a program that built further on those concepts was designed for supervisors.

The approach selected for the programs was an innovative one and was based on the following elements to help build an adaptive culture:

1. *Ownership and Responsibility.* "We all have customers to serve." Every member of the Canadian public is a customer of Canada Post. Employees had to hear and internalize the message that customers come first, whether they are members of the public or internal customers. In order to make employees active contributors to the survival of Canada Post, their belief systems had to change to include the concept of quality in service delivery, and they had to be encouraged to take ownership of it.

2. *Wake-up call.* Canada Post is facing increased competition from private courier companies as well as technology, and the expectations of customers have risen with the presence of these alternative services. No longer a monopoly, it must operate in ways that encourage customers to perceive higher value in using Canada Post's services. Employees had to understand a clear message about the changed competitive field and what it means to them personally in their day-to-day work.

3. *Employees teaching employees.* A deliberate decision was made to have the Service Plus programs facilitated by internal employees. This process allows employees to speak with other employees, rather than follow a more traditional model of having *experts* from the outside speak. Although employees may not be expert facilitators, they come with credibility, can understand fully participants' viewpoints, and are living models of commitment to customer service.

4. *Discovery approach.* To encourage a spirit of adaptability, a course design was chosen of presenting essential, but not overwhelming, information. A series of processes allow the participants to come to their own conclusions about the information, building their problem-solving abilities and encouraging them to improve service.

5. *Style and tone.* If continuous learning within the organization is to be achieved, learning must be an interesting activity. The program is designed to be interactive, kinesthetic, visual, physical, and fun. Learning activities are kept short and learning methodologies are varied frequently. The focus is on a team effort—making the group performance more important than the individual.

6. *Remove the barriers.* To increase significantly the speed of customer service—an adaptive response to increased competition—Canada Post had to remove barriers between customers and employees. Employees

needed to break the *we-they* paradigm and adopt a more inclusive one where customers become part of a new model.

Phase Two: Pilot

The Institute undertook a pilot phase in the fall of 1994 in six cities— Montreal, Ottawa, Toronto, Winnipeg, Calgary, and Vancouver. Over 900 employees took part in the two-day front-line employee program, and 100 supervisors took part in the four-day Leadership I program. The front-line employee perspective and the supervisory perspective, revealed by the evaluations, were as follows:

(a) Front-line employee perspective

Front-line employees typically receive technical training. Service Plus, which focuses on a shift of outlook and an increase in initiative as well as service skills, was a refreshing change. Sharing with them the full picture about the changing competitive environment and customer satisfaction survey results increased their ownership over the training results.

(b) Supervisory perspective

Acquiring leadership, team building, and customer service skills helped the supervisors grow personally. A custom-designed 360° feedback device, a significant departure for Canada Post, gave supervisors an understanding of how others perceived their customer service abilities. This mechanism drove the notion of internal customer, created a precedent for peer and subordinate feedback, and raised the level of self-awareness.

Phase Three: Train the Trainer

Starting in February 1995, the train-the-trainer phase began. Employees first attended the programs as participants and then took part in facilitator training. Participants were given the choice of presenting solo the first time or pairing with a colleague. This tactic enabled them to build their confidence in a safe environment before working on their own. Participants found ways to generate support and develop self-teaching mechanisms. Some groups organized lunch-time rehearsals of program segments; others used Toastmasters and similar venues to improve their presentation skills; and an informal tutoring network developed through the grapevine.

The internal trainers did well in their new roles and were pleased with the opportunity to expand their skill base. Most of them have expressed interest in being trainers for other programs the Learning Institute will sponsor. By the end of 1995, over 21,000 employees (38 percent of their workforce) had gone through the program. Through this first initiative, Canada Post has increased the learning potential of the organization. The bonus is the creation of an extensive network of change agents.

A participant concludes, "The success or failure of Canada Post is within each of us, and we must learn to get involved, know that it's the customer who puts bread and butter on our tables, and we cannot bite the hand that feeds us. The competition is fierce and the customer demanding, but we have the expertise to survive. All we have to do is put this expertise into practice. It's our future, let's make it good."

An Alternative Dispute Resolution Process

Canada, where capitalism co-exists with a concern for the common good, continues its history of strong unions. With their rights protected by legislation, unions have often been locked in adversarial confrontations with management. In the past, the price of these confrontations has been regarded as a cost of doing business. However, increasing global competition, and the resultant pressure on survival, has made that cost too high for both parties.

Alternatives to that cost are featured in this section. Adversarial behavior, because it has worked in the past, is hard to change and the way is not smooth. A crisis can result in slippage, and there can be several of these bumps on the road to permanent change. The journey, however, is worthwhile, as SaskPower has found.

SaskPower

SaskPower, the electric utility that serves the Province of Saskatchewan, like many other utilities in Canada, is being challenged by deregulation and other marketplace changes. Increasingly, customers are demanding a better deal since it is now possible for them to select power suppliers. These changes have thrown a spotlight on workplace restructuring and its impact on the workforce.

SaskPower embarked on a more collaborative approach to union/ management relations a few years ago. After experiencing traditional labor negotiations in 1992, both agreed they would like to approach their working relationship differently. As Kevin Mahoney, vice president of human resources, notes: "We all recognized—after spending almost a year in bargaining, getting a contract that basically offered nothing, and fighting over wording that nobody really cared about—that there had to be a better way."

The first seeds of cooperation were sown. Regular meetings allowed the open discussion of issues between union and management, and issues that were years old got resolved. Virtually all of the outstanding grievances were settled.

Encouraged by this promising start, management and unions then looked at other ways to do things collaboratively. One example was joint training and education. A small team of union/management representatives attended a program on cooperative approaches in the workplace offered by the Centre for Industrial Relations at Queen's University in Kingston, Ontario.

In 1994, union and management agreed to joint training in mutual gains problem solving and more than 200 employees received training. Both during and after the training, participants found they were able to use the mutual gains model to resolve real workplace issues and find new ways to approach problems.

In early 1995, building on the success of the mutual gains training, SaskPower decided to conduct an in-house *train-the-trainer* program. Thirty employees, a mix of union and management, received joint in-depth training over a five-day period on how to facilitate the program for other employees throughout the province. With this move, SaskPower was able to build internal strength in the mutual gains approach and signal that it was becoming part of the culture.

Also in early 1995, the organization embarked on a workplace restructuring whereby strategic business units were created as profit centers. Concurrent with this restructuring, it became clear that some downsizing would be required. Using a cascading staffing approach commencing from the top of the organization, SaskPower reduced its supervisory management positions by approximately 25 percent. In many cases this was achieved through redeployment, early retirement, and attrition.

However, as staffing was pushed down the organization, the union stressed the importance of using the collaborative mutual gains method for resolving concerns about in-scope positions. Representatives of both

Local 649 of the Communications, Energy and Paperworkers Union of Canada and Local 2067 of the International Brotherhood of Electrical Workers recognized the need for competitiveness. However, they reminded the company that utilizing the mutual gains process could lead to win/win solutions to manpower cuts. The result was a two-day collaborative problem-solving session held in Regina in September 1995, with attendance by the management team and representatives from both unions. Following this session, it was agreed that many union/management committees would be set up to further the dialogue and examine issues.

To this point, the way to change problem solving by a different method of working had proceeded fairly smoothly. Unfortunately, the timetable on the workplace issues was tight, and the President of SaskPower made it public that action must be taken by the end of 1995. This pressure evoked a concerned response from the unions.

Despite these pressures, no one is ready to abandon the mutual gains approach. All parties continue to dialogue, and the expressed hope is that win-win solutions to some very difficult issues can be found. The successes achieved over the last few years serve as a reminder that it is possible to reach a common view that can accommodate multiple interests. SaskPower shows that adaptive change is not easy, but a way must be found to accommodate it.

Transition With Dignity

During a time of organizational change, Ontario Hydro set up a career transition center to help their employees develop skills to find jobs and transition with dignity.

Ontario Hydro

Ontario Hydro, the major energy supplier for the Province of Ontario, had long been a destination employer, and had developed a culture of lifetime job security. Tremendous change occurred between 1993 and 1995 when it became necessary for approximately 7,000 employees (25 percent of staff) to leave Ontario Hydro because of the changing business climate. To meet the challenge, Ontario Hydro responded with a creative combination of early retirement incentives, voluntary buy-out packages, and gradual surplusing.

Everyone affected had the opportunity to partake in predecision counseling, financial advice, job search training, transition strategies, and even entrepreneurial grounding in launching businesses. Programming went far beyond legal requirements and industry norms and has been extended to include remaining employees still struggling with career issues.

Phase 1: Reorganization and Predecision Support

The major reduction in staff was driven by the need to restructure the organization and to reframe the focus of its business, as well as the desire to reduce overhead in order to remain competitive.

The first step in the process was, essentially, to abolish the entire structure of Ontario Hydro and eliminate every position. A new, streamlined structure was then announced and open competitions were held for all jobs at the executive and management levels. At the same time, a voluntary leave program was announced, featuring enhanced retirement and resignation incentives for anyone who wanted to exit the organization. People did not know if they would have jobs, what jobs those might be or, if they were even going to stay at all. Meanwhile, business had to continue to meet customers' demands for quality service.

Human resources' challenges were immense, and the time frame to address them was very short. A relatively small team of recruitment and training specialists was established as the Career Transition Centre, and consultants were hired to support them in strategy, program planning, and service delivery.

Several support programs were designed and implemented to assist employees through this confusing period. Workshops in resumé preparation and interview skills were directed at everyone competing for jobs in the revised organization. Detailed, individualized financial packages were prepared, outlining the terms under which employees could elect to leave. Group workshops explaining the financial formulas, entitlements, and tax implications attracted huge audiences, and everyone had access to personal financial counseling. Individual coaching around career options, lifestyle issues, and dealing with stress was made available to those who needed help in deciding whether to stay or go.

Managers in critical operating units were trained in techniques around managing change, in helping staff members make decisions, and, most importantly, in keeping productivity levels up during times of transition.

The window of voluntary leave options was kept open until all positions in the new organization (for which there were competitions) had been filled, so that unsuccessful candidates could either apply elsewhere or take the package. The bulk of positions at lower levels were filled through direct nominations by the new management team without the same competition process.

Phase 2: Career Transition Programming and Support

A fully equipped Career Centre for departing employees was set up in Toronto, base office for the largest concentration of staff members. It included resource materials, job boards, computers, classrooms, administrative assistance, and access to counselors. The Career Transition Centre proactively canvassed the marketplace to generate opportunities. Training programs were developed and offered to employees at 12 different geographic locations across Ontario. The training package for each departing employee included the following:
- A three-day comprehensive job search program.
- Six different supplemental half-day workshops, from a list of 14 available topics including networking, stress management, creative retirement, image, communication styles, and budgeting.
- A half-day of individual coaching.

Human resources had a tremendous administrative challenge to meet, while still delivering high quality in the programs. A special computer program was developed to field applications for training and to group requests by topic desired and geographic preference. A team of facilitators from Ontario Hydro was assembled and trained to help deliver the 15 workshops along with external consultants. Local human resources staff was trained on coaching and advising techniques to service exiting employees not able to access the main Career Centre. In some cases, smaller career centers were set up to support local needs.

Phase 3: Career Transition Programming Revisited

A year later, another round of downsizing was initiated, this time to smooth out the unevenness created within the organizational structure and to enact refinements in business strategy. The uptake to this voluntary leave opportunity was about 1,000 more employees; significant in most quarters, but only a relatively small project compared to the previous experience. The groundwork laid earlier, and programs already up and running, allowed this phase to be completed even more smoothly and efficiently.

However, final adjustments to staffing levels and structure could not be completed because the collective bargaining agreement now included a clause of employment security or no layoffs. Therefore, significant numbers of surplus unionized staff were granted employment security for the duration of the collective agreement (March 31, 1996) unless they chose the voluntary exit option.

Phase 4: Career Development and Retraining

The final phase involves those employees lingering on surplus lists, waiting to see if the next collective agreement would continue to protect them. Understandably, the organization was hoping to realize some productivity output from this group in the interim.

A process was designed to develop a Career Development component aimed at encouraging employees to assume a greater sense of control over their futures and to pursue retraining or other skills enhancement avenues actively. This initiative had to overcome a traditional resistance to change in a long-standing culture that designated the organization as primarily responsible for providing development opportunities.

Many people were either not motivated or had little idea of where to start in moving their careers forward—both to increase short-term productivity and to enhance long-term career mobility inside or outside Ontario Hydro. Business units within the organization that had a sizable surplus population arranged to offer special retraining allowances tied to the preparation of focused development plans. Managers were assigned to manage local programs, and the former Career Transition Centre became the new Career Development Centre. Workshops were developed and supported by individual coaching.

Typically, organizations pay a lot of attention to managing change— the mechanics of systems, procedures, tasks, plans, and controls involved in shifting structures and/or strategies. It is less common that organizations pay attention to managing transition—people implications, personal reactions, support needs, and individual differences that result from imposed change.

Ontario Hydro's attempts to balance these challenges required the ability to adapt to circumstances. Human resources was able to leverage the successes of each phase into the next and learned from what worked well and from their mistakes. The sheer magnitude of the project and the unwavering dedication to be caring and fair to employees stands out in this experience. Managing transition is never easy, but Ontario Hydro was creative and adaptive in making it as smooth as possible.

FUTURE TRENDS

Human resource departments that have focused on creating the adaptive culture realize that prepackaged, one-size-fits-all solutions no longer work. They see each problem and opportunity and each individual as being unique, and they search for unique solutions to create the adaptive culture.

The departments described in this chapter have developed a new set of competencies and cultures. They include a macro perspective on the new global marketplace, the ability to quickly assess people and systems, and leading-edge organizational management knowledge and information. They have changed permanently and will continue to do so.

To a large extent, Canadian organizations have reinvented themselves, and employees are coming to terms with this paradigm. To maximize the potential of people in new organizations, the mandate of human resources management in Canada is to become a strategic player in a process of renewal.

CHAPTER 2

United States

Beverly Forté, Vice President
Performance Systems Design
The Odenwald Connection, Inc.

CURRENT ISSUES

These last few years of the 20th century are changing U.S. companies in fundamental ways that challenge every aspect of their operation. The nature of these challenges vary along a continuum from radical downsizing to rapid expansion. To meet these new challenges, U.S. organizations are turning to training in new ways to facilitate change and continue to improve performance to achieve and sustain a competitive global advantage.

Several majors issues have predominated as a result of these changes. Perhaps the most pervasive issue has been the restructuring of the workforce into teams. Teams are increasingly required to cross boundaries at all levels of the organization—e.g., cross-functional, cross-location, cross-cultural. Although more of these self-managed teams are taking on tasks formerly managed by supervisors and managers, in 1995 only about one-third are considered self-directed.

Partnering is another prominent issue—partnering either *within the company* with other individuals, teams or departments or *outside the company* with suppliers/vendors, consultants, or other companies through joint ventures. The number of organizations partnering increased to 44 percent in 1995—a 10 percent increase over 1994. Also influenced by downsizing is the new trend of using more contingent workers or *outsourcing*. This use jumped from 14 percent in 1994 to 25 percent by the end of 1995. Other no less important issues are a continued emphasis on total quality management (TQM), developing corporate vision, reengineering, and benchmarking.

Because of the globalization of business, an increase in cross-cultural or global business training is also occurring. This transformation of U.S. companies from domestic to international organizations is leading to a whirlwind of ever-changing terminology, technology, and resources. This phenomenon has moved corporations to an emphasis on personal responsibility and improved performance—the push to deliver ever greater competence and productivity in the workplace.

An increasing number of U.S. companies are using competency models to more directly link individual performance to achievement of business objectives. Competency models provide a framework within which to respond to these issues by pinpointing what it takes to do a job exceptionally well. Identification of competencies begins with a simple premise: The best way to find out what it takes to do a job is to analyze the job's outstanding performers and then to study what they do that makes them so effective.

Assessment and identification of competencies should not be so much assessment of the job as assessment of the person who does the job. Job competency assessment is similar in theme to Peters and Waterman's *In Search of Excellence*: find out what the best people are doing and organize recruiting, training, appraisal, and other human resource management systems around the characteristics that separate the high performers from the others.

This approach is distinct from other theories or intuitions about what makes top performers because it is based on real people in real jobs. However, terms like "competency tests, "competency-based education," and "competency model" are often heard in the business of training and development but without generally agreed-upon meanings.

Training and development programs based on competency models are among the most effective programs available. One of the keys to the success of these programs is that the behaviorally specific competencies become the learning objectives of the training. Both the instructor and the participants can see whether the critical skills are being acquired because they can measure these competencies by the demonstration of the related behaviors. Further, since the competencies relate to effective job performance, competency-based training has a built-in rationale: acquiring the competencies will make one a more effective performer.

Three case studies will be used to provide examples.

Praxair Surface Technologies

Praxair Surface Technologies (PST), a global company with operations in nine countries, is a pioneer in the manufacture, invention and use of wear-resistant coatings and specialty powders, and jet engine fan blade repair. PST is a subsidiary of Praxair, Inc., the largest supplier of industrial gases in North and South America and one of the largest worldwide. In 1994, this successful company faced a probing question, "How can we advance our global, competitive advantage through our people?" PST began their inquiry by initiating a competency study process directed by Rex Heitz, director of human resources. This process had several advantages over the more traditional analysis of job requirements. It allowed PST to:

- Distinguish the competencies of the outstanding performers from those that are common to all performers.
- Get beneath the espoused theories about what it takes to do a job, to what their best performers actually do.
- Focus on the fewest number of competencies that make the most difference.
- Define competencies in terms of observable on-the-job behaviors.

The PST competency study process included the following activities:
1. Meetings were held with management and incumbent resources to obtain needed information via current documentation and performance data such as performance appraisals.
2. Critical behavior interviews were conducted on-site with identified workers in the United States, Asia, Japan, Singapore, and by phone to other worldwide locations. Top performing sales engineers, plant engineers, R&D engineers, team leaders, plant managers, sales managers, and business general managers were interviewed.
3. Following the interviewing and survey processes, competency models were developed based on identified competencies. Competency categories included conceptual skills, financial skills, global business skills, influencing skills, strategic planning, technical skills, and time and organizational management. The categories providing the greatest amount of input, involvement, and productivity improvement for the

company were designated as core competency categories. Others were then divided into subcategories that supported each of the core categories. For example, under the core competency category of communication, subcategories included coaching, interviewing, listening, presenting, relating to customers, and writing.

4. The competency models were validated and appropriate training and method of delivery (i.e., on-the-job training, self study, and/or traditional classroom training) were identified. PST took into consideration that the models must be defined as a set of operatives that would allow them to implement the interventions worldwide, regardless of location or type of product.

5. Appropriate interventions were generated.

The competency model was then linked to the business model and the career development model. According to HRD Manager Larry Ludwig, PST began this process by reviewing the existing company training which included OJT, self study, and traditional training courses developed internally or externally. Then they reviewed their performance appraisal process, strategic goals, and selection and development of past and current interventions. They also considered the area of career development in terms of what had been done in the past, what was perceived to be currently in place, and what people had indicated they wanted to have happen. Based on these findings and on the information from the competency study, a comprehensive transition plan was developed to ensure successful implementation of identified interventions. This plan included prioritization and scheduling of identified training needs and determination of whether training would be internally or externally developed and delivered. PST identified core competencies and curriculums for technical management, organizational, and professional development. It is important to note that not all interventions identified during the transition process involved training.

In 1996, PST will continue the transition process in parallel with implementation of new interventions identified. Implementation requires a thorough understanding of current organizational processes and identification of new processes that need to be in place before implementation of the integrated career development competency model. This may require changes in performance appraisals and career development discussions, methods of collecting documentation about training and development and other areas of employee development. For example,

PST must examine how the information is currently kept (e.g., is it on paper, can it be put into a HR software package). All options must be considered before implementation.

There are several other issues for PST to consider during the implementation phase.

- Champions must be selected within their organization to help identify potential departments where interventions can be applied, either in a pilot environment or where the acceptance level will be high enough that they can get accurate evaluations and measurements of what they are doing well and what needs further development. The key to success with this kind of activity is to keep it as simple as possible without compromising the necessary functions for implementation.
- When the actual interventions are implemented, PST must have methods to document and evaluate the process to ensure timely interventions.

One of PST's ongoing goals of the entire process is to maximize achievement of both organization and employees goals. PST will continue to provide opportunities to increase productivity of the organization and the employee by using the competency model in conjunction with the business, training, and career development models. At all times, it is important to strive for congruity between the needs of the organization and the needs of the employees. PST's task is to allow both to move to their maximum limits. Coordinated career development between the organization and the employee will insure the best possible situations for both. People selection and development as well as customer focus become important issues.

Advantages of interconnecting required competencies with organizational and employee goals include: shorter cycle time for learning; better organizational development; increased commitment; targeted and more effective budget expenditures; self-directed employees with less intervention. This enables HR to function within the business strategy more effectively and makes the process a transparent tool rather than the focus of effort.

PST is already beginning the process of aligning their models and processes to ensure success of the whole system. They are reviewing their performance appraisals and career development systems, how they collect performance data, who will collect data, and how it will be made available for managers so they can use it appropriately. They are having to look at one-, three-, and five-year development plans. As a result, they need data such as the longevity of their people in terms of how long they stay in a job function and work for the company and the people's succession needs compared to the company's growth rate.

It is important to note that it is not always possible to secure additional human resources for job functions. As a result, the process which transitions the focus from the competency model to the career development model is essential to leverage the employee's contribution to the organizational goals.

In summary, the effective study and use of competencies takes a person-centered approach to defining the behaviors that relate to outstanding job performance. It begins as an analysis of individual top performers and ends as a redefinition of human resource management. The competency models that are produced serve as the tools for developing human resources in the present and as the instrument for charting the organization's future. They specify critical characteristics to guide hiring and performance appraisal; they define training objectives; they encourage self-development; and they provide guides to matching people to jobs. Employees become dynamic participants in their own careers, facilitated by the organization.

The benefits to the organization of a competency-based human resource management system are numerous and significant. The obvious benefit is individual and organizational productivity. A competency-based system enhances the management of people by all who make decisions in hiring, placement, and development. With competency models for the jobs of greatest strategic importance, succession planning and early identification of high-potential performers become possible as never before. And finally, a competency–based system provides organizational coherence: it links individual competence to performance measures and performance measures to organizational goals. With the right people in the right jobs, the organization is positioned to achieve its mission.

SmithKline Beecham

SmithKline Beecham (SB) is a U.K.-based pharmaceutical company with R&D headquarters located in Upper Merion, Pennsylvania. SB's strategic intent is to become "The Simply Better Healthcare Company." Many of the strategies SB is pursuing, such as business integration, process management, cycle time reduction, and disease management required advanced computing and information management as a core competency to be successful. This challenge places a great responsibility on SB's Information Resources (IR) function.

IR is meeting the challenge by implementing a Competency Development Process which is designed to raise the bar of proficiency across the worldwide Information Resources (IR) community. The focus of the project is to enable each person to become a superior performer in their current role to raise the proficiency of the whole IR function, while, at the same time, encouraging the development of transferable skills which can be used in any future roles an individual may undertake. According to John Parker, senior vice president and director of IR, the project has two clear goals:

- To support the overall goal of building a world-class IR organization by identifying the critical competencies that enable superior performance for IR professional staff.
- To develop and implement a strategy to increase the degree of these competencies throughout the IR Community worldwide.

IR Competency Development is designed to be a complementary process to the Leadership and Development Review process. Each was developed independently but for similar purposes. Together the two processes ensure insightful focus on development within IR and equivalent representation of its people in the company-wide planning and review process.

The project team defines a competency as a complex combination of skill, knowledge, practical know-how, motivation, and other personal traits that has been shown to describe or predict outstanding job performance in a given role or situation. Competencies are considered characteristics, which, if developed, lead to visible improvements in proficiency. For example, a core IR competency is Business Partner Customer Orientation (i.e., knowledgeable of the business and oriented toward providing business solutions to benefit client unit).

To identify IR competencies, the organization, with the assistance of consultants, carried out a series of in-depth, confidential interviews with incumbents in different positions within a specific job family from all IR groups in the United States and the United Kingdom. The information gathered was analyzed and coded so that the competencies demonstrated by effective and superior performers could be identified and categorized.

Competency models were then developed to identify the skills and behaviors of superior performers in six job families, which covered most technical professional positions across IR. The job families were: Analyst Programmer, Technology Specialist, Manager IR Services, IR Services Specialist, Consultant/Accountant Manager, and Project Manager.

Tools and resources were developed to support the implementation of the project. These included model descriptions and development planning forms, competency-based interview guides for use in selecting candidates for a given job family, and educational materials and programs designed to support personal development. To minimize the amount of paper generated in this process, software was developed to support the project. This system enables forms to be completed and exchanged electronically and development plans to be constructed and monitored on screen.

The Competency Development Process is designed to be an employee-driven process. It provides a systematic way for individuals to identify current strengths and development needs and to formulate a development action plan. Managers can benefit from the process by using researched competency models both as a basis for developing and raising the levels of performance of current staff and for recruiting new individuals into their organization.

The Competency Development project has already been rolled out in the company's Technical Management Services (U.S. and U.K.), Corporate Systems and Services (U.S. and U.K.), and Consumer HealthCare (Pittsburgh, Pennsylvania). During 1996, the implementation process is gathering momentum, with the company committed to ensuring that there is measurable progress over the next year.

Motorola Advanced Messaging Systems Division Paging Products Group

Motorola is one of the world's leading providers of wireless communications, semiconductors, and advanced electronic systems and services. Their rapid rate of expansion worldwide has presented new challenges in accelerating the new employee's ability to perform effectively. To facilitate this process, their Advanced Messaging Systems Division of the Paging Products Group in Fort Worth, Texas, has recently implemented an innovative, performance-based training program for their New Employee Orientation. Developed by Charleen Allen, training manager, the orientation consists of several components:

- Pre-Work (with video tape)
- Two-Day Orientation
- Orientation Passport (to be completed within the first ninety days of employment by all new associates and transferees)
- Structured On-the-Job Training (OJT) Checklist (for specific job categories)
- New Employee Notebook

Pre-Work

The Pre-Work consists of all the paperwork that must be completed including benefits decisions. The paperwork is accompanied by a videotape that includes a welcome by the Human Resource Director, an explanation of the purpose and use of the video, directions for the forms, a brief history of Motorola, and an explanation of benefits.

Two-Day Orientation

The Two-Day Orientation presents an overview of Motorola culture, values, beliefs, ethics, and key initiatives, and provides an opportunity for the associates to tour the facility and the factory.

Orientation Passport

The Orientation Passport, which looks like a real passport, provides new associates with a tour of the various elements that make up the Advanced Messaging Systems Division (AMSD) within the Paging Products Group of Motorola.

Being a global company, Motorola saw similarity between the first ninety days of employment within a company and a trip around the world. There are different stops along the journey that are important for the new employee to understand the values and culture of the organization. There are also specific tasks that must be completed to ensure that the company infrastructure operates properly.

The Orientation Passport was created to guide the new associate's journey. Each page of the passport specifies a task category with several action items that must be completed within the first ninety days of employment. Associates are empowered to accomplish these items.

Managers do not closely track the completion of each item during this period. Instead, each item is signed off by a designated mentor when the task is accomplished.

At the ninety-day mark, the associates meet with their managers to review progress. When all items are accomplished, the manager signs-off and sends the passport to Training where it is filed in the associate's personnel file. The associate then receives a $50 value card (money card to be used in the facility for food and snacks).

Structured On-the-Job Training Checklist

The Structured On-the-Job Training Checklist is one of the items listed in the Orientation Passport. When the program was initially implemented, there were checklists for positions within Manufacturing, Engineering, and Information Systems. Additional checklists in the areas of Order Entry, Sales and Marketing, Finance, Human Resources, and Clerical positions throughout the division are planned. Each checklist has a list of performance-based tasks that must be completed within the first ninety days of employment. The checklist is reviewed by the manager at the same time as the Orientation Passport and, when completed, is returned to Training with the Passport to be filed in the associate's personnel file.

New Employee Notebook

The New Employee Notebook contains the materials presented in the Two-Day Orientation. It also contains relevant information for new associates in the area of
- Motorola Initiatives.
- Introduction to Motorola, Paging Products Group, and AMSD.
- Human Resources and Training.
- Security and Protection of Proprietary Information Guidelines.
- Computer and E-Mail information and guidelines.
- Communication.
- E-Money (Electronic Expense Reimbursement System).
- Information on the city for associates new to the area.
- Yellow Pages of phone numbers sorted by topic instead of a person's name.
- Appendix of forms and pages to be completed and turned in.

In addition to a paper copy distributed at the Orientation, the New Employee Notebook is available on the Motorola network in an electronic version that has hyperlinks to each item in the Table of Contents for ease of access to the needed information. It is formatted in Adobe Acrobat and is put on the internal network and in a Web Page on the Internet for easy access.

FUTURE TRENDS

In a December 1994 report of the National HRD Executive Survey conducted by the American Society for Training and Development, almost all survey participants believed that training expenditures would continue to increase over the next few years even though the training emphasis and role of training would change over this period.

In 1995, U. S. organizations budgeted $52.2 billion for formal training according to *Training* Magazine's *Industry Report, 1995.* Not adjusting for inflation, this figure is a 3.2 percent increase over 1994. The report also reveals that total dollars budgeted for outside expenditures—such as seminars, computers and packaged training programs—is $10.3 billion, a 4 percent increase over the previous year.

According to the *U.S. Industrial Outlook 1994,* public and private expenditures for education and corporate training accounted for nearly eight percent of the gross domestic product (GDP) in current dollars in 1993 and were predicted to increase by nearly $530 billion (6 percent in 1994).

A total of 49.6 million individuals received some formal training from their employers during 1995, which represents a 26 percent increase since 1990. Likewise, the number of training hours delivered by U.S. organizations with 100 or more workers has increased by 24 percent over the past 5 years. In a September 1994 Bureau of Labor Statistics report, 71 percent of the 12,000 private businesses surveyed provided training for their employees.

Who receives the most training within U.S. companies? The largest training budget amount—54 percent—is spent on managers and professionals, sales personnel receive 14 percent, while the remaining third of the training budget—33 percent —is spent on training for other employees (e.g., production workers, service personnel, and administrative staff).

Although training emphasis varies by industry, training in basic computer skills is the most offered training across industrial categories— 93 percent of employers offer computer training according to *Industry Report, 1995.* In addition to technical training, other popular topics listed are:

- New employee orientation
- Performance appraisals
- Leadership
- Sexual harassment
- Team building
- Safety
- Hiring/selection process
- Train-the-trainer
- Decision-making
- Listening skills

- Time management
- Conducting meetings
- Quality improvement
- Delegation skills
- Problem-solving
- Goal-setting
- Managing change
- Motivation
- Stress management
- Diversity

The hottest training topic on the *Industry Report, 1995,* list of topics is sexual harassment which moved from No. 17 in 1994 to No. 5 in 1995. Diversity training will continue to increase along with more emphasis on ethics and values. There is also a new focus on responsibility, accountability, and spirituality in the workplace.

Work itself is being rethought, from being the drudgery of earning a paycheck to being the gratification that comes from meaningful work. Because of a need for balance, employees are looking for more meaning out of their work lives as well as their personal lives. Corporate CEOs will talk intently about corporate soul as a reflection of the 1993 bestseller, *The Soul of Business* by Tom Chappell. There is a growing evidence that value-driven companies outperform their competitors, according to Terrence Deal's *Leading with Soul: An Uncommon Journey of Spirit.* Since jobs come and go, more people will begin to ask, "What's my work in life? What's my contribution to society?" There are an increasing number of companies offering seminars for their employees to deal with these emerging issues.

According to ASTD's 1994 National HRD Executive Survey, management development, customer service training, and technical training will receive the most attention in the next few years followed by organizational development, sales training, quality training, and career development. This report also listed some of the major concerns and issues HRD will face in the immediate future.

- Measuring bottom-line payoff of training.
- Doing more with less.
- Adapting to the emerging technologies.
- Executive support for training.
- Managing an increasingly diverse workforce.
- Providing alternatives to classroom instruction.
- Downsizing.
- Helping managers move from a *training* mindset to a *performance improvement* mindset.
- Transfer of training.
- Identifying and improving basic workforce competency.
- Globalization.
- Accelerating the learning process.

Three major areas that will increasingly affect American training efforts in the next 10 years are: technological innovation, globalization, and the changing role of the training function.

Technological Innovation

In recent years, technological innovation has fostered considerable change in manufacturing processes. Significant automation and an increase in the use of computer-related technology have caused workers—who were once considered to have sufficient skills for lifetime employment—to learn new skills and processes to sustain their employment in an ever-changing environment. One-fourth to nearly half of manufacturing industries including industrial machines, fabricated metals, electronic instruments and equipment, and transportation equipment manufacturing now use computer-aided design and computer-aided engineering in their overall operations. Many of the companies in these industries also use computer-controlled technology on the factory floor.

Among the trends in computing that will affect the use of technology and training are:
- Optical data storage.
- Digital electronics.
- Smaller, more powerful computers.
- Networks with distributed computing such as Internet.

These technologies will provide new training methods that will allow self-paced training at individual workstations or even at home. Companies will also extend their computer technology and training to customers and suppliers.

Globalization

The demands of international competition and a multicultural workforce will continue to change the way U.S. businesses are organized and operated. Long distance communication and information networks will blur corporate and national boundaries even more than today.

Because of today's emphasis on specialized information and expertise, teams of full-time employees, consultants, partners, and outsourced workers will be responsible for the design of key processes and projects worldwide. Global requirements will necessitate specialized training in negotiation, decision making, and problem solving for all team members.

As the diversity of the U.S. workforce steps up, training will play an increasing role in helping workers understand cultural differences. Companies must learn how to incorporate diverse values, ethics, and workstyles into their practices, products, and services while preserving the underlying beliefs, values, and ethics of their corporate culture. For American-based multinationals, this will also necessitate an increase in training for employees and joint venture partners outside the United States.

The Changing Role of the Training Function

Corporate trainers will spend less time in the classroom and more time partnering with internal customers and managing external providers. Training instruction will continue to shift from training professionals to line managers, team leaders, and technical workers. More training will be delivered through technology, just-in-time, or directly on-the-job in an effort to make learning more relevant and to reduce training time required away from the job site. Trainers will become coaches and problem solvers, and many companies will hire a Chief Knowledge Officer (CKO) who is responsible for the dissemination of information and learning. The future will provide difficult but exciting times and opportunity out of chaos for the training profession.

CHAPTER 3

Central America

Serge Ogranovitch, President
The Potomack Partnership

CURRENT ISSUES

During the last half of the 1980s, to help create jobs and develop a growth-oriented climate, most of the Central American governments were busy attracting multinational entities. During that period and the early 1990s, the training and development focus of the multinational was on technical, job-specific skill building. In 1993, this trend began changing to include supervisory and managerial skills. The goal of corporations also has shifted from bringing in expatriate managers to developing local managers who understand both the corporation's managerial style and the home culture.

For the most part, the technical skills building training has been offered by using North American training programs, barely adapted to the local environment. In the case of European or Asian corporations, the programs were delivered by corporate trainers using a variety of programs from North America or their own country. Most programs were *Made in the USA*, and delivered by local trainers either in English with simultaneous translation or in the local language.

The multinational corporations brought with them the concepts of total quality management (TQM), empowerment, team building, and delegating. These concepts were implemented by the corporation through either internal instructors or consultants brought in by the home office to promote the corporate management culture in the new environment. The programs, for

43

the most part, ignored the local cultures and were not compatible with local values. The training program designers lacked the ability or understanding needed to help both the corporate and local people to understand each other and adapt the materials to fit the new environment.

As a result, a large percentage of the management and supervisory training has failed, while the skills training, mostly provided through hands-on and *buddy* type programs, has been successful in developing an excellent task-oriented loyal workforce. These programs, due to the nature of close contact with the people, developed the necessary sensitivity to the environment and were adapted enough to be effective.

Thus, the main problem faced by trainers delivering programs in Central America has been the program's lack of cultural sensitivity and the trainer's unfamiliarity with the environment in which they were working.

In the past several years, local universities, the Young Presidents Organizations (YPOs), and business development organizations—both private and government sponsored—have started providing training and management seminars. The majority are still delivered by consultants from other countries with little cultural sensitivity. Most are lectures with few, if any, practical applicability in the workplace. The emphasis is still on using university professors with little practical on-the-job application.

Instituto Interamericano de Cooperación para la Agricultura

Instituto Interamericano de Cooperación para la Agricultura (IICA) is a part of the Organization of American States. Thirty-three countries are members of this not-for-profit organization. The purpose of IICA is to foster agricultural development in the member countries through technical and financial assistance. In early 1994, IICA offered a three-day executive management workshop on Managing for Excellence (MFE). This course reviews seven skills that assist busy executives to better manage their organizations.

The members of the IICA group in Barbados that participated in the MFE program were country managers for the Caribbean Region. Like most organizations in technical areas, IICA's managers were first technical experts and second, managers. Eight nationalities were represented in the class, with the obvious different cultural values and management styles. In many instances, the skills the course presented were new to the participants. In other instances, the participants had learned the skills through on-the-job experimentation. As is the case in many such programs, the skills participants wanted the most assistance with were communication, delegation, and team building.

A few weeks after the Barbados seminar one of the participants, Ms. Jan Hurwitch, the Country Manager in Haiti, requested some assistance in Port-au-Prince. The first task she wanted to focus on was team building for her local IICA organization, and the second was to assist IICA's effort in supporting the Minister of Agriculture—appointed by exiled Haitian President Jean Bertrand Aristide—on decentralization plans for the Ministry of Agriculture. So, Serge Ogranovitch of The Potomack Partnership led the seminar and concentrated on the human resources aspects of decentralization. Since the return to Haiti of President Aristide, the Ministry of Agriculture has embarked on a decentralization program, and the first training program on decentralization has taken place. With regard to team building, Ms. Hurwitch had already started team-related activities and was delegating to her staff, and needed very little assistance except for reinforcement of some skills.

At the IICA headquarters in San José, Costa Rica, during that same time frame, a new IICA Director General was being elected. After the election of the new Director General, an interactive program on management skills, team building, and strategic directing was planned for IICA's management staff.

Background

The group consisted of the top management of this highly political organization, including the Director General. The board of directors of the organization consists of the Minister of Agriculture or the equivalent from each of the 33 member countries, so the 25 to 30 participants were from 11 different member nations. While all professed to be totally and only dedicated to IICA, it was soon evident that individual national interests and cultural values had a big impact on how individual executives managed and communicated.

The Director General, Dr. Carlos Aquino, wanted to instill a Participatory Management style in the organization. An extremely gifted visionary, he asked that the program direct the participants toward that management style.

Dr. Aquino felt that participatory management would improve the organization's response to its clients. Also, many of the programs presently managed by headquarters personnel could then move to the field, closer to the local clients. He also wanted the heavily centralized organization to decentralize, so the country managers could develop the ability to make more decisions and, therefore, become more responsive to their clients. The issue of more local decisions and more responsiveness to local demands was one of the main complaints of the country managers in the Barbados MFE program. The country managers felt that decisions from San Jose were too slow and that headquarters staff did not have the same understanding of the local situation that they, being on location, did. Decentralization also meant to Dr. Aquino that responsibility and authority needed to filter down to lower levels of management and that all IICA employees should have input into the organization.

To most executives at IICA, Participatory Management meant very different things. Dr. Aquino had inherited an executive staff that had been appointed by his predecessor, and in most cases they had not been in favor of his election to the post. To the *old guard,* his ideas of management and in particular the *participatory* concept were frightening. To most of them, it meant that they would lose control over *their* part of IICA and lose *their* organizational power. After spending years in a very strong hierarchy, they found it difficult to voluntarily change their management style, especially when it was not a part of their cultural values.

Culture had a great deal to do with the management problems Dr. Aquino was facing since the cultures of the top executives had a direct impact on how the organization functioned. Different cultures controlled different parts of the organization, and each member had established unofficial networks. The top management group in the course were from Argentina, Brazil, Canada, Chile, Costa Rica, Cuba, Dominican Republic, Peru, USA, and the West Indies.

The challenge was to design a team-building, culturally sensitive program that would explain what participatory management is, obtain support for it, and at the same time build some common managerial skills.

The Program Design

The first requirement was to come up with an event name that would not be too threatening to the participants and make them want to attend. So an *executive retreat* for the top executives was planned away from the office at a secluded resort on the outskirts of the rain forest near San José. Second, the program needed to attract not only the top executives that were to participate, but also to address the needs of the middle management level who reported to the executives. In the end, middle management was easier to sell on the need for this program. Knowing that this meant that they would have more impact on the organization, they welcomed the opportunity to participate. So, in addition to the executive retreat for top managers, two half-day sessions were designed for the middle managers. The sessions for the middle managers took place the day before the retreat at the IICA offices. The first half-day session was on culture and its impact on communications. The second session concentrated on team building and using teams effectively. The two sessions were so successful with middle managers that the word filtered up to the executives, and it gave the retreat a strong enthusiastic start.

To achieve Dr. Aquino's goals for the retreat, the program included the following topics:
- Participatory Management.
- Vision/Mission.
- Goals and Objectives.
- Culture: What It Is and How to Use It.
- The Effect of Culture in Management.
- Building Multicultural Teams.
- Time and Time Wasters.
- Setting Priorities.
- Problem Solving.
- Listening and Communication.
- Feedback and Coaching.

The final session involved all participants in developing and sharing an action plan for implementing Participatory Management in their part of the organization.

The decision was made to make this three-day program as participatory as possible. The methodology used in the design emphasized the participants' involvement in many interactive activities, forcing them to work through problems as team members, effectively using Participatory Management. That decision would eventually be the most important design step to what became a very successful program. It allowed them to see for themselves that Participatory Management works and provides for better communications and decisions. Another key design decision was to have long training days. The participants became more involved as the days went by. Discussions started during the class day and continued at dinner.

The materials and the exercises were multicultural and emphasized the effect of culture on decisions and how each participant saw the problem(s) and solutions in accordance with his or her cultural values and biases.

Implementation

With participants from so many countries and languages, simultaneous interpretation was used for the retreat and the two half-day seminars. Several hours were spent with the interpreters, reviewing the materials, exercises, and their roles. Whenever an instructor uses interpreters, clarifying roles is important. The instructor needs to clearly understand whatever the participants say—not just what the interpreters think the participants meant to say. At the same time, translating exactly what the instructor is saying is also important. In this case, interpreters' skills and patience added value to the programs. The participants spoke English, Spanish, and Portuguese, and while most could speak either English or Spanish, they could not express all of their thoughts in the other language(s).

The first session for the middle managers addressed the fact that IICA has several dominant cultures within the organization and that not everyone thinks alike and works in the same fashion. They needed to learn about individuals' cultural values, the differences between the values, and how to use this understanding to more effectively work as an organization. Also IICA's clients, the 33 countries, have different cultures and values that need to be integrated into the planning and implementation programs. During the session, the 100 managers participated in exercises to identify their own individual cultural values and used the results in small groups to resolve a problem.

The second half-day session concentrated on forming and managing teams. IICA had started project teams a few months earlier and was finding that, for the majority, they were not working well. Top managers wanted to dominate and, as a result, the middle managers were not participating.

During this session, exercises were used to illustrate how teams, especially multinational teams, can work and how to set up teams and manage them.

Building on their descriptions and views of Participatory Management, the 100 participants looked at definitions of top-down versus bottom-up management styles and expanded the discussion to define Participatory Management in a way that all could understand.

Then they discussed the official Vision and Mission of IICA and how to set achievable goals and objectives.

That led to a review of the need for

- Understanding the impact of culture on management and marketing strategies.
- Learning how to use culture for sales, corporate strategies, and management structures.
- Understanding the skills needed to function in a multicultural environment.

Following a definition of culture, the group assessed their own individual cultures and looked at ways to better understand and adapt their skills to function effectively in the other cultures.

Delegation—Using Multicultural Teams

The session first explored how participants felt about delegation and the use of teams. Then they looked at the complex issue of managing and motivating multicultural teams in the context of team logistics, leadership, and communications.

To implement change, participants looked at how decisions are made. As they saw during the time management module, not all decisions are made based on contribution to one's job. However, all decisions good or bad start with a set of assumptions, feelings, and attitudes toward the decision that needs to be made. They then focused on what is important, what the problems are, what the choices are, how each choice contributes, and which is the most important.

The second day also included Problem Solving. Since the definition of *problem* varied from culture to culture, they defined *problem* and reviewed a six-set model:

1. Define the problem.
2. Rule out the areas that are working (i.e., what is not a problem).
3. Identify what is unknown.
4. Make a list of what the problem could be.

5. Look at each of the *could be* items to determine if it is causing the problem.
6. Select the most likely cause of the problem and identify what action(s) need to be taken to solve it.

The final day was centered around the topics of communication feedback and coaching, and the development of the participants' individual action plans. The key to effective management is the ability to give feedback, positive (praise) or negative (criticism), in a constructive fashion. Feedback is telling someone how they are doing, and coaching (a form of feedback) is helping employees work through particular personal problems that are affecting their usually good performance. However, feedback is very difficult when used across cultures.

No program that professes to develop participant managerial skills is good unless the participants are able to use the skills in real life situations after the program. The goals of the program were to expose the participants to Participatory Management and give them skills to become better managers, and to help them implement Participatory Management. This last session discussed the importance of developing and implementing a Participatory Management plan.

The next step for IICA's top managers is to continue building on the communications and delegation skills acquired during the retreat and the two half-day seminars. This can be easily achieved by building skills at the middle and lower management levels, and by continuing to promote participation in management and decisions at all levels of the organization.

To further this growth, the organization has put in place several new communication tools to help with participation at all levels. A series of training programs has also been a model for various levels of the organization.

FUTURE TRENDS

During the early 1990s, the region has undergone a tremendous political change. More democratically oriented governments are seen throughout the region, including the election of a president in Haiti, his ouster and reinstatement, a more western orientation in Cuba, as well as the continuing strengthening of democracy in other countries of the region. Most regional governments are actively seeking multinational corporations and making it attractive for them to come and invest in their countries. The telecommunication industry is rapidly moving to a private service provider system to increase communication quality, making it easier for corporations to work globally. Governments are looking at telecommunication technology with a clear understanding that the countries that provide good quality, dependable telecommunication services at reasonable prices will attract the multinational corporations. In the training field, they have also realized that developing—at the technical and university level—good skilled managers is essential for building an infrastructure that will support a modern technology-based global marketplace.

In the training environment, several differing trends are taking shape through the Central American region. Multinational corporations have discovered that what may work at home may not be effective locally, and the *think globally, act locally* idea works and needs to be emphasized. As a result, local companies will increase

- The number of adapted training programs that are geared to the audience at hand.
- Their investment in management planning and staff development, using modern techniques and programs.
- Their use of more practical experience-based training.

The skills programs are going to continue through both technical institutes and in-house programs. The level of education in most of Central America is increasing and a larger percentage of the population is moving into the middle management ranks through either formal studies or through company-sponsored development programs.

The following trends are emerging in countries like Costa Rica, Honduras, Barbados, and Trinidad:

- Better skilled managers can act locally as well as be effective members of global organizations.
- Computer technology is making it easier for middle managers and upper-level managers to catch up with—and often surpass—the managers from the multinational's host country in the new skills learning curve.

Most new managers in the region have not gone through centralization/decentralization, reengineering, TQM, or just-in-time concepts. The new skills they are learning are fresh, and—when the training is adapted to the cultural environment—they are quickly absorbed and implemented.

The Central American region is quickly developing as a global center for industries from around the world using the *work-smarter* thinking process rather than the *work-harder* method of past decades.

CHAPTER 4

South America

Hugo Nisembaum, Director
HN Education & Performance

CURRENT ISSUES

A *new time* has emerged in South America—especially in Chile, Argentina, Brazil, Paraguay, and Uruguay—countries that form a *natural* and now more concrete common market (Mercosur). Political and economic stability and an open and global economy brought to South American companies—both multinationals and nationals—a new approach to training issues.

South American companies have always been in contact with the most known programs in the training field, but due to local instability and discontinuity in the training effort, they were often seduced by *quick fix* programs. Even when the Quality Era arrived, many companies insisted on short-time vision and efforts. Now the difference among those who really understand that they are competing in a global market is readily evident.

A permanent investment in education is becoming a recognized need and is affecting the way programs are developed. This is part of a new paradigm that assumes that
- There are no quick fixes.
- Significant problems require analytical solutions.
- A long-term view is needed to bring about meaningful results.

For example, Management Development has always been an important issue. The way those Executive Programs are implemented today, however, is quite different.   Clear linkage to corporate strategy is a must, and continuity and modularity are other important characteristics. A systems approach and integration with other human resource efforts are also more prevalent. Performance Appraisal, Talent and Potential Appraisal, 360° Feedback, Self-Assessment, and Assessment Centers are often added to the executive programs.

Partnerships with local and international universities are a growing trend, and specific projects are a part of the training programs. Corporate Strategy, Marketing and Sales Strategies and Management, Finance and Economics, and Information Technology are always found in some form in these management development programs.

Other very common topics are those related to Total Quality. Quality tools have become a common language (either Japanese, American, or European with local adaptations). Customer Service is also a key issue.

Team Management, Self-Directed Teams, and Team Performance are integrated parts of new organizational structure and architecture. Outdoor Training is often used as an approach to teamwork. Computer-Based Training and Multimedia are gradually being introduced. An increased interest is seen in these programs, especially from those who include consistent learning concepts in their development and application. Rapid change can be expected due to demands to accelerate competency curves while decreasing expenses and limiting overhead. On-line Knowledge is expected to come from powerful interactive advisory systems. Performance technology and performance support will be one of the key development issues also.

Trainers are changing the way they think and work. Becoming an internal consultant and developing new skills are part of specific training programs for this new role. As internal consultants, they will have to add new learning tools to their competencies and answer a fundamental question: "What business are we in?"

In the area of Sales Training, with programs stressing Customer-Oriented or Consultative Selling, there is also a clear trend to view management and supervisory roles as coaches for the sales team and more effort of field and on-the-job learning experiences. Information technology is increasingly used as sales support systems. As a natural influence, Performance Team/Sales Teams are more usual.

Competing globally also accelerates the need to develop Expeditionary Training Missions. Participation in international seminars and guided visits to foreign companies are a part of training programs, too.

Amil—Health Care and Assistance

Amil was founded in 1979 and is today one of the main health care assistance companies in Brazil. In 1994, it expanded into the United States and Argentina. Growing fast and being different are part of the Amil way of doing things. Their particular market approach helped to develop a different way of relating to human resources, training, and education.

Amil's vision is to be the biggest and best company through satisfied people—including employees, suppliers, and clients. With this in mind, Amil presents itself as a *high-tech/high-touch* company.

Continued education has always been considered a key factor for success and has oriented actions not only for their employees, but also for suppliers and clients. The Amil Group is convinced that growth comes through knowledge. For this reason, in 1993 they established the *Escola Amil de Administraçao* or Amil Business School. This corporate (virtual) university is responsible for the educational programs for employees, suppliers, and clients. With their suppliers (physicians and hospitals), they developed a special relationship, sponsoring seminars for the medical class and offering research support.

Clients and prospects are one of their target groups for international conferences on Management and Health Care Management. And for their employees, the human resource strategy stresses three points: people development, career opportunities, and motivation through challenges. The concept of *Learning Manager* is literally used at the Amil Business School where 80 percent of their teachers are internal. Each manager commits to a minimum of 40 hours a year of teaching at the school. They believe that knowledge can grow when individual experience is shared throughout the organization.

Corporate training is oriented and coordinated by the Amil Business School, a strategic and centralized effort. Operational training is coordinated directly by area managers and is decentralized and tactical. Each employee participates 18 days a year in training/educational events (not including operational and on-the-job training). The following programs are examples of this training.

Year 2000 Amil Seminar

Vision, commitment, group action, and culture and common values are key issues in this seminar. Every trimester, the CEO and top managers discuss and analyze Amil's strategies and study together new management concepts that can be useful for the company. An interesting gallery of national and international books are part of their learning dialogue.

International Seminars

Amil put together *in company* seminars combining their top executives and clients for an exchange of new ideas and business concepts. Peter Drucker, Regis McKenna, Richard Whiteley, Michael Porter, Claus Moller, and Karl Albecht were speakers at those seminars.

Amil Service Seminars (ASE)

Aware that quality service is achieved when the complete service cycle is engaged in the quality effort, the Amil Business School introduced a series of seminars targeted to a para-medical audience. The issues developed were Customer Service, Win-Win Relationships, Service Quality, and Customer Expectations.

Amil Business Administration (ABA)

This is a 300-hour-per-year program developed for managers, coordinators, and other professionals with university background. It works like an internal masters degree program. Key subjects include health care systems, quality, products and service development, corporate strategy and vision, negotiation, finance, people management, marketing, and decision making. Those *Internal Learning Managers* introduced into the classroom a very interesting mix of theory and practice. Seven courses were presented for 200 managers.

Amil Selling Administration (ASA)

Specifically for sales people, this 200-hour program considers that a good salesman is the one who has not only sales skills but also a global knowledge of marketing, the economy, writing skills, presentation skills, and the health care system.

Learning Organization Meeting

Looking for an opportunity to improve transfer of learning and a way to promote networking among their employees, these meetings can include discussion of issues like Medicine in the United States, presenting conclusions of an Executive Study Tour, Culture Change, or Strategic Marketing. The meetings are open, participation is spontaneous, and the sessions become a vehicle to encourage change from the bottom up.

Partnership Development

With their medical suppliers, Amil implemented the Scientific Support Program (SSP), and through this program they take charge of diffusion of medical information coming from the key medical magazines and distribute it to 2,700 physicians monthly helping to develop 800 searches per month.

"We need a workforce enabled with knowledge and skills as fast as we can. A workforce aligned with strategy that knows more, can do more and will do more," affirms Telmo Pereira, Human Resource Manager at Amil. The Amil Business School is there to help and enable the knowledge sharing. Learning comes from formal events, experiential events, and internal and external relationships.

Integration of educational programs with other human resource systems is a must. They developed and installed a Performance Appraisal process (Can/Will). This process offers a more objective way to evaluate, establish a commitment, develop an individual education plan, and define what contribution is expected for better performance and action planning. The Can/Will instrument works with two basic categories: will (commitment, enthusiasm and initiative) and competencies (related to leadership and technical skills). Amil's managers link their success—financial, market share, service quality—to their training effort.

For Amil, the challenge is to build a world-class workforce and the instrument is the Amil Business School. This corporate university follows the five core principles model presented by Jeanne C. Meister in her book *Corporate Quality Universities:*
• Link training to the strategic needs of the business.
• Train the entire customer/supply chain. This includes key customers,

product and service suppliers, and schools who provide tomorrow's workers.
- The curriculum incorporates corporate culture, contextual framework, and core competencies.
- Consider the university model to be a process rather than a place.
- Experiment with new ways of learning and postlearning reinforcement.

For Amil, becoming a multinational company is a learning process—not just a growth strategy. Being in a global market, learning the best practices, showing their service quality and testing their practices in those markets are fundamental. So they decided to start operations in the United States in 1994. The Mercosur (South American Economic Common Market), including Brazil, Argentina, Uruguay, and Paraguay, is part of Amil's strategic plans. Being in Argentina is crucial since it is second in size to Brazil in the South American market.

Paulo Marcos, Amil chairman for Argentina, compares training in Brazil and in Argentina and comments that since Argentina has better formal education than Brazil, the focus for training in Argentina is operational training. Issues like teamwork, motivation, and empowerment are very important. Cultural differences are also interesting. Argentineans are more individualistic and hierarchical, and those cultural differences are important since Amil employees in Brazil work more in teams, with a circle organization, and with increased job rotation.

Unibanco

The largest private bank in Brazil, with more than 764 branches (agencies), decided to make significant changes in the way they do business. The competitive advantage achieved is the result of a new corporate strategy defining the bank structure in Business Units and Service Units. According to this new strategy, a new manager profile was necessary. Better results with increased autonomy and responsibility is a characteristic of this new *business manager* profile.

Excellency Management Program

The Excellency Management Program (PEG) was created to answer this strategic business need. This program is structured in three stages and addresses all levels. The program presents and discusses bank mission, objectives, strategy, managers' new profile, and performance support tools for excellence.

Unibanco's Manager Posture was defined and, accordingly, managers should do the following:
1. Be in charge of their business.
2. Be in charge of human resource management.
3. Look for innovation and work improvement.
4. Stimulate exchange and interaction with all levels and relationships internally and externally.
5. Invest in professional and personal development.

The manager's profile attributes are responsibility, loyalty, initiative, creativity, decision making, communication, relationship, and entrepreneurship. This organizational redesign process and adaptation to a new culture required different strategic positions and actions from the Human Resource Department. Decentralization of human resources and training issues were one of the results. Human resource professionals took over the new role of internal consultants working as a part of a service unit, developing products and services for their internal clients.

PEG was one of their new products. This corporate program is considered today as one of the key contributors to Unibanco's profitability. This program focuses on actions that are client oriented and serves as a fundamental cornerstone for professional development—a tool to implement the new Unibanco Manager Profile.

With *PEG's* introduction came a new way to treat training issues. Unibanco's managers are now responsible for identifying their team training needs (including self-assessment training needs), and they are in charge of their training budgets.

During Stage I, Unibanco's chief executive officer and vice presidents were directly involved, and they established the link among the new market strategy and the new profile needed for implementation. Impact was very significant. Participating and discussing openly with top management was a clear message that demonstrated that decentralization was there to stay.

Stage II worked on the definition of the new profile with the participation and contribution of 950 bank managers. At the same time, the new HR and Training role was discussed and defined, and action steps were taken.

Stage III communicated the changes for all 20,000 Unibanco's employees. This is part of a permanent effort to communicate the bank's mission, objectives, strategy, and the new manager profile to all business and service units. Stage IV includes updating and maintenance, with continuous involvement of the CEO and Managers. This stage is used as a forum to discuss how to participate and communicate on a regular basis with all employees and transmit new corporate challenges and changes.

PEG is used as an Umbrella Corporate Program to spread or propagate bank culture and values. One of the programs under the *PEG's* umbrella is the Development of Technical and Managerial Excellence (Sidex). This program integrates all the new competencies and establishes a curriculum for the new profile. The training consists of three modules: (1) Corporate, (2) Specifics for Business or Service Units, and (3) Supplementaries. These segments are flexible, even having a logic order, and adaptable to managers' individuals needs. The Corporate modules are mandatory for every manager.

Subjects developed within each module include

1. Corporate
   - The Role of Business or Service Units in Market Strategy.
   - Planning, Management and Control at Unibanco.
   - Negotiation.
   - Leadership.
   - Performance Appraisal Systems.
   - People Management.
   - Internal Communication as a Management Tool.

2. Specific for Business or Service Units
   - Examples, according to Need.
   - Knowing Your Business and Products.
   - Knowing Your Competitors.
   - New Profile Management applied to Business or Service Units.
   - International and National Financial Systems.
   - Advanced Bank Management Program developed specifically for the Retail Bank Units.

3. Supplementary
   - Bank Marketing.
   - Foreign Languages.

To complete these efforts, International Seminars called *With an Eye on the World* bring global concepts to internal discussions.

All of these programs were developed through partnerships established with universities and consulting firms and were created according to bank needs and culture. This concept of customized education assures that workers are being prepared with the skills and competencies needed for the future.

Recently, Unibanco introduced several appraisal tools to complement the programs. The first instrument introduced was the Performance Appraisal System, which links managers' goals to company goals and evaluates the manager in terms of results, production, and quality. Application and review occur twice a year.

Aware that Performance Appraisal is more related to compensation items, the Talent or Potential Appraisal was developed to better identify their managerial human resources and afford opportunities for their managers to maximize their potential. This Talent Appraisal provides development and maintenance actions for strategic human resources, supports succession planning, and helps to fill key positions in the organization.

The two appraisal tools allow Unibanco to administer their talents and strategic human resources *individually*. They can cross the needs for new positions with available talent. That is the Performance and Talent Appraisal Mix. According to this mix, employees will receive more specific compensation plans and training investments.

Another way to increase managers' awareness of their own professional development is through a Management Excellence Appraisal. This appraisal allows anonymous input from a manager's subordinates. This type of evaluation is not mandatory but gives the managers a profile of how they compare to other bank managers. This is not a 360° feedback instrument, and they understand that, culturally, the introduction of these kinds of tools takes time to implement. However, it is clearly perceived that human resources has moved to a new and more strategic position in the bank and is now present at key meetings. A more proactive approach is present, and human resources professionals are looking for business opportunities to contribute actively to business goals.

These programs have certainly helped to build the new manager profile. Managers are now expected to take charge of their self-development in a more proactive manner. New paradigms in career development are needed to elicit new ways for managers to look at and progress in their careers.

Quality at Unibanco is oriented and coordinated by the Academia de Qualidade Unibanco. This academy is responsible for the quality education process, for training facilitators and quality internal consultants, and for helping to create tools for quality implementation. Managers, in the new role of *owners of their business,* are deeply involved in the process as facilitators. They were trained for this role and, through their example, help to introduce quality concepts and instruments in a very pragmatic way. Each area discusses their standards and measurement indicators and the ways that they can measure. Continuity, speed, and evaluation are essential for implementing the quality process. They believe that not being *enchanted* with quality theories was fundamental and, as a result, their approach is practical.

They learned about quality by implementing quality. The quality process is deeply integrated with *PEG* and with the new role of bank managers as human resources managers of their teams. Programs such as *People Management* reinforce the quality approach through people. The Academia de Qualidade Unibanco is now developing a system for recognition, ways to reinforce quality standards and performance, so that it translates into lasting improvements in individual performance and collective learning for the organization.

An example of training decentralization is the Retail Training Department. They are looking for new learning methods, and their main challenges are learning by doing, assuring transfer of learning into job experiences, being more in contact with field reality, providing more short-term training programs, reducing classroom hours, and increasing on-the-job learning experiences.

Also, human resource consultants are deeply integrated in a redesign process developed by the bank, working on new positions, feeding trainers and program developers with new competencies needed for new jobs. Inplacement and reallocation are easier now with appraisal tools already introduced. This also demonstrates that the new proactive posture of Human Resources helps to manage change before it occurs and in a preventive way. With all these integrated actions, Unibanco is more prepared for competitiveness with a better trained workforce, which is creating a high-performance work environment.

Avon

Avon is a multinational U.S. cosmetic manufacturer with plants in Brazil, Argentina, and Chile. They also have business units in Peru, Bolivia,

Ecuador, Colombia, Venezuela, and Paraguay. Avon's vision is "to be the company who best understands and satisfies the product, service, and self-fulfillment needs of women globally."

Times are changing at Avon. They expect an income of US$ 1,000,000,000 for 1995, 23 percent more than 1994. Sales are growing, and new plans for human resources development are coming in a new way. In their opinion, human resources was not considered strategic for the organization. Bureaucracy was central and the company concluded that the way training was used did not answer real needs, did not have added value, and resulted in the loss of time and money. They were, as they admitted, *experts* implementing imported or local training packages that did not respond to business needs.

Many programs (e.g., Education for Quality, Service Excellence, Time Management) were implemented in the 80s as an exclusive activity of Human Resources, and the idea of internal clients was not used. They were training for activities, not for results or performance improvements.

Simple programs, such as integration of new hired, were not developed with *real* responsibility for their integration, according to the needs of each area. Resistance to being results oriented or to measuring performance was due to lack of specific strategy for Human Resources and to *know how*.

Today, Avon is starting a new Human Resource model, and a Strategic Human Resource Plan has been developed. Their new vision is "to be identified as a business unit inside the company" and the HR Strategic Plan addresses three fundamental points:
• Business growth.
• Responding to customer needs.
• Building competitive and advantage.

This new model is based on different roles and relationships between the human resource development (HRD) and their partners. A partnership established between HRD and Managers is one of the key issues. To get out from behind the *Expert on Training and HR* and become an Internal Consultant working with the client/manager/employee is the major challenge, and an educational process has begun to teach both sides what can be expected from the new approach and how the actions can be implemented.

Process Education teaches the new skills needed for internal consultants: understanding the business and defining the business need, clarifying expectations and contracting, selling (programs, recommendations, and ideas), leading change, taking stock, and sales closing are a number of skills practiced in the new approach. Partners should be approached with a strategic perspective, and teamwork is the rule of the game.

Brazil has begun this internal consultative approach—more in touch with operations and customer needs. Other South American Avon bases will analyze the model and see how they can apply it to their countries.

Today education and training programs are delivered differently. Avon's definition of *core competencies* are a "global map" for human resource development. Investment in training and development is customized locally and includes a clear identification of individual needs. On-the-job learning or learning by doing is also a part of the training plan, and managers are responsible for adequate environment conditions.

Performance Development Process was introduced in 1995. This is a part of an Avon global human resource process. The project in Brazil already has a new look since managers are involved from the very start. This new tool was introduced through Performance Management Seminars for managers and supervisors. Key issues of the program are:
- Self-performance and team-performance analysis
- Better understanding of business strategy and values and their influence on actions and their impact on performance
- The career development process
- Coaching and feedback
- Training needs for the future related to company challenges

This Performance Development Process emphasizes teamwork. Each manager has individual goals, but also a minimum of two common goals with another manager. In this way working together is constantly reinforced.

Many other companies like Avon are changing the human resource role. Success in this process will depend on:
1. Alternatives forms to deal with bureaucracy (A heavy weight in the area).
2. Alternative ways of learning, understanding them and presenting them to the partners.
3. Educating the partners. (If the managers are responsible for their human resources, they need to know more about dealing with that issue.)
4. HRD and managers together must contribute through their joint effort with performance improvement.

FUTURE TRENDS

Work is changing, and as a result, training approaches need to shift in the same direction. What is already seen as a significant trend is that training is redefined from a one-time event, targeted to one's internal employees, to a process of lifelong learning including a company's customer/supply chain as well as their internal employees.

With the permanent redesign of organizations, learning to run the individual's career as a small-business venture and the competencies related to this new situation is, and will continue as, a focus of learning. The role of human resource professionals is also changing as they become more like agents managing a pool of talent programs, giving to Career Development a broad view and a new set of skills to be learned.

One of South America's problems is adequate basic and formal education, a well-educated workforce is a must for competitiveness. Some evidence is appearing that organizations in this geographic area are taking charge of this educational gap, not waiting for a government solution. Universities are initiating a more significant partnership with private companies. An increasing number of organizations are creating their own corporate universities in a clear demonstration of, and commitment to, life-long learning. New approaches to workforce education (either one-on-one or small groups) are needed to teach a wide range of job-related skills, while diagnosing specific learning needs and problems. Since the new economy stresses continuous learning, employees also will have to increase their ability to learn how to learn.

In a knowledge economy, knowledge capital must increase, and as a result of this, companies will request on-demand, just-in-time learning experiences. Development of interactive instruction using computers and multimedia devices will grow steadily.

Managers will be more involved as Learning Managers and will have to become more familiar with the learning process and how to create a positive learning environment.

Businesses will need new approaches to training and development because complex tactical and strategic tasks now require the assimilation of large amounts of new knowledge and heavy workloads. These approaches will have to provide sequentially arranged, systematic, applied workplace training for individuals and small groups.

Organizations are identifying their core competencies—what is the actual gap and the curriculum needed (formal+experience on the job) to conquer competitive advantage. New individual skills are a necessary condition for new organizational capabilities, but they are not sufficient to guarantee the development of such abilities. Organizationwide learning will require critical masses of individuals operating in new ways and will require new infrastructures that support learning. Those infrastructures may be Performance Support Systems, Performance and Learning Consultants (internal or external), Corporate Universities, Learning Teams, Common and Alternative Learning Methods, and Self-Directed Learning. Performance and Learning Management will be a competency mix highly requested. As Peter Block says: "Learning will be the only job left to managers."

The entrepreneurial spirit is going to be intensified, with the help of the information superhighways and high technology. Organizations made up of autonomous teams with marketlike freedoms need effective processes for everyone to participate in shaping the bigger picture. Empowerment will continue as a key issue.

The people of South America are living in a new democratic era, and the democratic process fosters commitment and responsibility to shared goals. Learning democratic processes is as vital to a transition to a more intelligent organization and country as are individual and team business skills. The Latin individualistic approach will need to become more group oriented. Working with people to reduce selfishness will be one of the biggest challenges and the only way to change the environment.

Fluid structures will have to provide feedback for on-the-job development and continuous learning. Different appraisal tools will continue to be used. But must of all, the South American people will have to change a strong paradigm still in use—from working *harder* to working *smarter*. That is what the global market demands: competitiveness, flexibility, quickness, core competencies, quality, and high performance.

REGION 2: EUROPE

CHAPTER 5

Western Europe

Wolf-Dieter Gebhardt and
Alexander Mutafoff
hr TEAM international

CURRENT ISSUES

This chapter does not identify case studies from specific companies. It discusses how personnel development in Germany is undertaken and demonstrates that companies by and large follow this procedure to get the best from their human resources.

These concepts have been applied in whole or in part with such leading companies as Draegerwerke AG, Volksbank, GMAC, and Dresdner Bank. Perhaps the concept shows features that might be of even broader interest to companies operating internationally.

In 1990, research showed that more and more companies found it difficult to get qualified personnel in spite of the fact that in Germany (and this stands for the rest of Europe, too) there are approximately 3.5 million people out of work at that time. Three reasons were identified as causes. The first reason is that there are not enough highly qualified people around who can meet the job demands now and into the third millennium. The second reason is that many enterprises do not present themselves in an attractive way to the labor market. The third reason is that enterprises usually do not have a systematic analysis of the potential they need and do not provide development of the potential. This leads to the fact that they need to, but often cannot, recruit successors out of their own environment.

The competition to win qualified employees will increase within the next years, particularly through the Maastricht treaty across the EU. Therefore, to get the leading edge, more companies now are deciding to turn to strategic personnel development.

Personnel development, as a process to ensure current and future company success, has become a leadership task with top priority. From our consulting experience, we know that personnel development as a permanent process can only be implemented in a company if it is actively supported by the top management.

Personnel Development

Definitions

Personnel development increases employee technical competence, decision competence, and social competence in accordance with the company targets and philosophy. Personnel development must be closely linked to company philosophy, which means that by necessity the values and the targets of the company must be considered in the process. The particular personality should be developed to fit a perceived debit. If a company's values are partnership, customer satisfaction, and reliability, it will develop individuals differently from a company whose values are flexibility, aggressiveness, and dynamics.

Company philosophy comprises all of the values and norms and is, therefore, the guideline for the actions of the people within that company.

Company culture, the sum total of the values and norms actually lived by the people in a company, contains also those peculiarities and behaviors that are not desired but still shown.

Company targets are the measurable results that a company wants to reach in the future.

Interlocking Systems

Any company operates as an interlocking system, an organization of a multitude of factors that are dependent upon each other. Personnel development is influenced by company culture, company philosophy, company targets, the market situation, the legislative, training and development, and leadership style. All of these factors need to be considered before any development can take place (see Figure 5.1).

Personnel Development Process

Company leadership and management must competently handle continuous change and use human resources for a positive company image and future success. Today, virtually all companies are vividly aware that the most important image and success potentials rest in the employee. It is top management's duty to develop, advance, and use such potentials.

If personnel development is understood as a process, the company must not only constantly react in continuous change, but also develop itself on the basis of expected future trends. Change within the working environment can be met by continuous personnel development, an important tool of entrepreneurship.

Company Philosophy and Company Culture

Leaders need to strengthen employee identification with the company, its targets, and its philosophy. The norms and the values of the company philosophy, therefore, are the basis of all activities and instruments applied in personnel development.

Company Targets

The company targets have a critical influence on personnel development. Personnel development goals for most companies include the following:
- Using the full potential of employees.
- Increasing the attractiveness of the company internally and within the market.
- Raising employee continuity and morale.
- Internally increasing employee qualifications.
- Improving the dialogue with employees.
- Gaining leadership succession out of one's own resources.

Market Situation

The market situation, with its life cycles, influences company strategy and personnel development. Whatever strategy the company is using—whether an investment strategy, a skimming strategy, or a retreat strategy—the strategy requires different personnel profiles for management.

Figure 5.1
Personnel Development Process

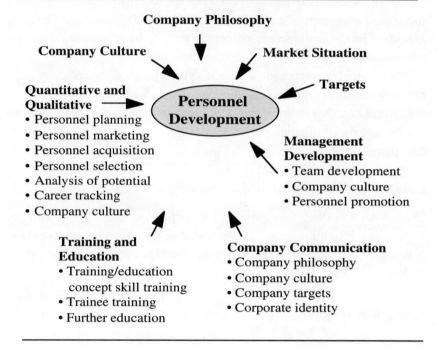

Company Philosophy

Company Culture   Market Situation

Quantitative and   **Personnel**   Targets
Qualitative ──────▶   **Development**
• Personnel planning
• Personnel marketing
• Personnel acquisition   **Management**
• Personnel selection   **Development**
• Analysis of potential   • Team development
• Career tracking   • Company culture
• Company culture   • Personnel promotion

        Training and   **Company Communication**
        Education   • Company philosophy
         • Training/education   • Company culture
           concept skill training   • Company targets
         • Trainee training   • Corporate identity
         • Further education

Areas and Instruments

Personnel development primarily touches a company in the following four
sectors:

1. Quantitative and qualitative personnel planning.
2. Training and education.
3. Leadership development.
4. Company communication.

Personnel development supports the company strategy by a variety of activities in each of these areas.

Quantitative and Qualitative Personnel Planning

Personnel planning—as a system of personnel marketing, personnel selection, and quantitative and qualitative staff planning—has to contribute in reaching the personnel development targets. To reach qualified personnel, personnel marketing will necessitate running company showcases or public relations activities.

The importance of personnel selection increases through tougher legislative requirements and continuously increasing personnel costs, which subsequently increase the risk of malselection. European companies increasingly choose elaborate selection methods, like assessment or development centers, to minimize that risk.

Personnel planning includes age structure planning. Ideally, the company continuously has a sufficient number of staff. So companies develop human resources to have a functional personnel cycle from the first day of employment and training via skill building and career tracking right through to retirement.

Activities and instruments include
- Succession planning
- Career planning
- Job rotation
- Personnel development programs
- Integration plans

Training and Education

Based on the training concept and the company strategy, medium- and long-term training activities are being bundled in a training strategy for skill areas, for behavioral areas, and for training junior staff. Apart from the need for company-oriented training, specific individual learning needs must be considered. Training and education, in this case, is not just a mere offer, but it is a need-oriented, long-term, and planned development of the company's human resources.

Training activities and instruments include
- Training needs analysis
- Training concept
- Training strategy

- Seminars and workshops
- Training on the job
- Trainee programs
- Education controlling

Management Development

Management development aligns employees and their abilities to job requirements to reach defined targets. The development should be conducted so employees' needs are respected and continuous support is given so that employees can access all their abilities on the job.

Management and personnel development are closely connected since the manager depends upon the achievement and development of co-workers. Personnel development assures success for the company, develops a positive company climate, and ensures that the individual keeps up with developments and job requirements.

Managers are asked more than ever before to lead and develop teams and promote cooperation within the entire organization (concept of the internal customer). Any development and promotion programs for management have to focus specifically on strategic competencies. That means that managers must be trained in discovering and exploiting of chances. This is being tried not so much by learning from mistakes in the past, but rather by learning from the positive developments and thus getting a positive future-oriented directive.

Management development activities and instruments include the following:

- Seminars for managers
- Coordinators' conference
- Coaching
- Leadership behavior analysis
- Management guide

Company Communication

Company communication, the internal official and unofficial flow of information, is the structure of cooperation within a company. Most often, the interaction between people is more important than the structural organization. Company communication and company culture serve as a frame for company strategy as a whole and strategic personnel development.

At least for Germany, the development of company culture will be one of the most important management tasks in the near future. Dynamic and self-assured co-workers who will take on responsibility and empowerment will expect to be led in the future more and more by visions and clear purpose. Therefore, leadership will be regarded as the ability to implement agreeable value systems and allow co-workers more entrepreneurship and more self-control.

Communication activities and instruments include
- Personnel development within company communication.
- Company newsletter.
- Roundtable sessions.
- Staff questionnaires.
- Working paper on company philosophy.

Instruments in Personnel Development

This section introduces some examples of instruments used in personnel. Figure 5.2 presents an overview of personnel development instruments.

Figure 5.2
Overview

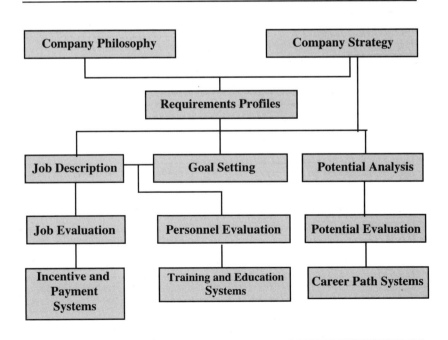

Job Descriptions

A job description is a formalized written statement of all important features of a job. Apart from its multiple use within personnel, the job description is important within personnel development. Job descriptions are being used for the following purposes:

- To decide on desired qualifications of job applicants.
- As a basis for applicant's selection.
- To integrate new employees into their job tasks.
- To help in the evaluation of employees.
- As a standard for job requirements and objectives for the job owners.
- To determine qualification deficits and to decide qualification activities accordingly.
- To develop career paths.

Figure 5.3
Job Description Form

JOB DESCRIPTION	
Organizational unit: **Department:**	**Name:** **Position:**
Job name: **Objective of the activity:**	
Position within the organization: [Superior] [Job owner] organization chart	
She/He supervises:	**She/He is supervised by:**
She/He deputizes:	**She/He is deputized by:**
Tasks and responsibilities: **Remarks:**	**Responsibilities:** **Internal Communication:** **Informs:** **Is informed by:**

In a system of job descriptions, the employees have a clear view of the possibility of personnel development. Together with job profiles, they are the basis for the selection of applicants and the qualification of achievers. Figure 5.3 shows a sample job description form, and Figures 5.4 and 5.5 focus on requirement profiles.

Requirement Profiles

Several possible uses of requirement profiles are
- Supplementing job descriptions.
- Planning of personnel development activities.
- Support of the general personnel planning process.
- Personnel marketing and personnel advertising.
- Support in personnel deployment planning.

Figure 5.4
Uses of Requirement Profile

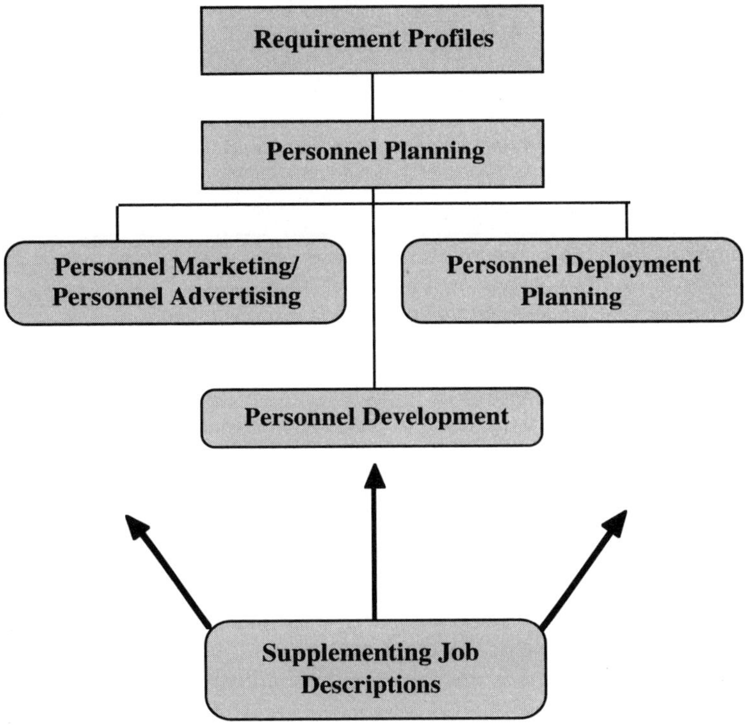

Figure 5.5
Structural Variances

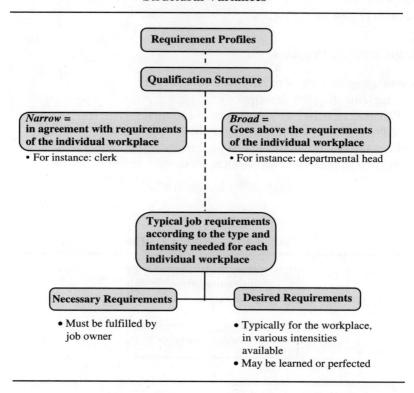

Requirement features (see Figure 5.6 for a sample job profile):
- **Identifiable features** are in agreement with the job descriptions and serve the explicit identification of the role.
- **General requirements** are personal characteristics of the employee (e.g., age, gender).
- **Knowledge features** (professional knowledge) are requirements for education, professional and further training, professional knowledge, and technical skill, as well as job experience.
- **Mental requirements** (thinking and expression) indicate the intelligence required of the employee.
- **Behavioral features** (job behavior/cooperation) are related to the work and social behavior required of the employee.

- **Leadership abilities** (leadership behavior) – are related to the leadership or management behavior.
- **Physical requirements** show any strains that may come from the job itself or the job environment.

Figure 5.6
Job Profile for a Sales Representative

Identifiable Features	• Job Name: sales representative retail trade • Department: sales • Income Group:_____
General Requirements	• Age: _____ • Gender: _____ • Nationality: _____
Knowledge	• Education/study: college/university (MBA) • Professional education: job training • Professional experience: a minimum of three years in sales required

Intellectual Requirements	1	2	3	4	5
• Communication ability	▭	▭			
• Analytical thinking	▭	▭			
• Flexibility in thinking and acting	▭	▭	▭		
• Creativity and ability to generate ideas	▭	▭			

Behavioral Requirements	1	2	3	4	5
• Self-directedness	▭				
• Responsibility	▭	▭			
• Dynamism	▭	▭	▭	▭	
• Ability to cooperate	▭	▭			
• Commercial ability	▭	▭			

Leadership Abilities	1	2	3	4	5
• Leadership motivation	▭	▭	▭		
• Goal setting, planning capabilities	▭	▭	▭		
• Ability to organize	▭				
• Ability to delegate	▭	▭			
• Ability to control	▭				
• Personnel development capabilities	▭				

Reasons for Evaluation Systems

The structure of the system to be introduced depends on targets that are reached by the personnel evaluation (see Figure 5.7 for more details).

Structural Variance

Figure 5.7
Reasons for Evaluation Systems

Targets	Importance				
	- -	-	o	+	+ +
Aid for achievement-oriented salaries					
Training need analysis					
Information for day-to-day personnel decisions					
Evaluation of the efficiency of activities within the personnel policy					
Instrument for motivation and leadership of employees					
Uncovering the achievement expectations of employees					
Advising and developing employees					
Praising and criticizing of results					
Enhancing the cooperation between management and employees					

Features of Evaluation Systems

- Evaluation systems should be based on the philosophy and the strategy of a company.
- Evaluation systems must harmonize and complement other instruments of the personnel development.
- Evaluation systems must be easy to handle to be fair in the results.
- Evaluation systems should aim the highest possible objectivity and should concentrate on measurable results. Figure 5.8 outlines the components of Evaluation Systems.

- Such subjective influences as sympathy and antipathy should be excluded as far as possible.
- Individual criteria and rating scales should be described very clearly in order to reduce the interpretation possibilities by the evaluators as well as the evaluated to an absolute minimum.
- The evaluation system must afford a regular or irregular evaluation (e.g., in transfers at the end of an assignment, promotion).

Free Statement of Impression

- Usually without much formal instructions, personal impressions about the behavior relevant to the success is being expressed by informal communication.
- Since it does not really fulfill the criteria of objectivity, reliability, or validity, it generally does not permit any objective comparison between employees.
- It is tightly connected to the ability of the manager to observe behavior and give clear behavioral feedback.
- It allows the exclusion of problem situations.

Rating System

- Categorization of behavioral observations and personality traits into multidimensional scales.
- The scales are generally expressed by figures.
- Evaluation dimensions generally are so freely formulated that they may serve a high variety of the workplaces.
- More sophisticated: behavior-related scaling on the basis of job analysis by method of critical incidents. This enhances the validity and acceptance; unfortunately, also, the effort in construction of such scales.

Example: Availability of Skills

The employee has the necessary skills for the job and uses such knowledge and his experiences accordingly.

Importance of the job function   Rating of employee

1	2	3	1	2	3	4	5

Further evaluation criteria may be

- Thinking and expression
  - Analytical thinking
  - Flexibility
  - Expression
- Job behavior
  - Job organization
  - Job readiness
  - Assertiveness
  - Job precision
  - Profit orientation
- Cooperation
- Leadership behavior
- Evaluation of total performance

Figure 5.8
Structural Variance

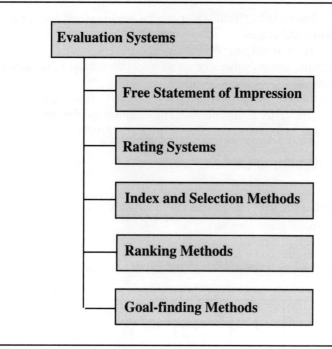

Index and Selection Methods

Description:
- Catalogs with a variety of features or behaviors are being used. The evaluator then either marks the field relating to a specific expression that fits the employee or he writes in a few words his observations of comparable behavior.
- Examples: Mixed statement list with multiple choice, group statement list with forced choice following the methodology of critical incidents.

Ranking Methods

Description:
- As general evaluation or differentiated by achievement areas.
- Where ranking is achieved by pair comparison, reliability will increase.
- Often suggested quotas are being used (i.e., 10% / 20% / 40% / 20% / 10%).
- This is expected to avoid varying standards of judgment and the tendency toward averages.
- Problems: Forced choice and zero sum games. This often reduces the acceptance.
- Target of behavioral ranking: For each person an ipsative ranking is developed. This does not put the person into a ranking scale but the persons' behaviors according to the degree of their relative appearance. Additional comparison of achievement can be obtained by so-called *sequential procentual ranking scales.*

Examples of a ranking method:

Please put employees into an order by which in your opinion they contribute toward achieving the departmental targets:

Employee rank 1:
Employee rank 2:

. . . .
. . . .
Employee rank n:

Goal-Finding Methods

1. Description:
- Combine motivation and performance development with performance evaluation.

- Derived from the company targets for each person, work or performance targets are described or agreed upon as well as criteria on how these may be reached. At the end of a specific time period there should be a performance evaluation as a comparison between the debit and the actual.
- Enhance performance.
- Targets should be short-term and clearly stated. Behavior-related goals are better than mere output (result goals).
- Participation in defining goals increases commitment.

Example:
Discussion of the areas of responsibility of the employee.

2. Which tasks and goals were the employees' main responsibilities during this time period?
   Task/goal 1:

3. Report on the results
   To what extent has task/goal 1 been fulfilled?
   Particularly good or poor results have been caused by:

4. Future tasks/goals in the area of
   Which tasks have to be managed?

5. What are the tasks for the employee resulting from this?
   Task/goal 1:

Description:
   Criteria for reaching the goals:
   Agreed performance standards and time scale:

Analysis of Potential

The analysis of potential aims at the future personnel development need of a company rather than the focus of the employee evaluation, which actually looks at the current qualification of the staff.

The analysis of potential unveils the entire development potential within a company in relation to all employees, the various levels of the hierarchy, or individual employees. It is thus a basis for future-oriented personnel development (see Figure 5.9).

The development potential of employees is the sum total of all the abilities, knowledge, and talents from which their suitability for additional or more difficult tasks derived (see Figure 5.10).

Features of Development Potentials

1. Learning and personal development
2. Potential of cooperation
3. Leadership potential
4. Judgment
5. Ability to organize and control
6. Readiness for responsibility
7. Potential of interest

Structural Variance of a Potential Analysis

Figure 5.9
Structural Variance of a Potential Analysis

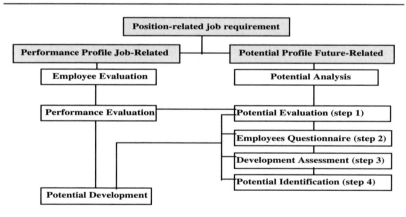

INSTRUMENT	IMPLEMENTATION BY	TARGET GROUP	TIME SCALE
Potential evaluation	Superiors	All employees	Annually
Employee questionnaire	Personnel department	All employees from selected divisions	Biannually
Development assessment	Personnel department	Junior management	According to requirement annually
Potential identification	Personnel department and supervisors	Superiors, leaders with potential for top management	According to requirement biannually

Evaluation of Development Potentials

The evaluation of potential is complementary to the evaluation of an employee's job performance. The former looks into future development possibilities whereas the latter looks at and includes past performance.

There are a number of inherent advantages. On the one hand, this indicates for employees that both managers and the organization as such are considering the individual's development and potential. This leads to a clearer and more realistic appreciation by the employee of development and career chances. On the other hand, it prompts managers to seriously consider, in an ongoing process, personnel development as an important part of their job role.

Figure 5.10
Evaluation of Development Potentials

The following evaluation format is used:
5 = has proven abilities and has shown their application
4 = shows good potential that needs focused development
3 = has potential, but needs support and development
2 = currently shows only few areas of development
1 = currently shows no development potential
Example: Development potential for ....

1. Willingness to learn and develop potential. Actively improves qualification to meet future challenges. Increases ability to master new and changing tasks.	1	2	3	4	5
	Development activities:				
Examples/remarks:					
2. Cost consciousness	1	2	3	4	5
	Development activities:				
Examples/remarks:					

Employee Questionnaires

The aim of presenting questionnaires to employees is to get information about and focus on their development needs. The employees have the chance to self-directedly voice their development expectations while the personnel department gets an overview of those potentially interested (see Figure 5.11 and Figure 5.12).

Figure 5.11
Questionnaire for Your Personnel Development

First name and surname:		
Profession:	Date of birth:	Date of joining company:
Marital status:	Nationality:	Personnel no.:
Job/Department/Division:		
Professional Development		

Employer	**Job function**	**From - to**

Institution	**Country/Place**	**From - to**

Topics	**Institution**	**Month/Year**

Education

Figure 5.12
Specific Skills and Experience

Interest in Development:

1. Production		3. Personnel	
1.1		3.1 Administration	
1.2		3.2 HR development	
1.3			
		4.	
2. Sales			
2.1 Complaints department		5.	
2.2 Sales presentation			
2.3			

Interest in Specific Job Functions:

1.
2.
3.
4.
5.

Personal Qualification for Job Function:

1.
2.
3.
4.
5.

Preferred Countries/Regions:

1.
2.
3.
Definitely exclude:

Assignments Abroad:

Very interested	
Depends on circumstance	
No interest	

Learning Needs:

1. Language

2.

Cultural Awareness Training:

1.

2.

Specific Skills and Experience

I ask for a meeting on my personal development:

☐ yes   ☐ no

Development Center

Advantages And Objectives

Development centers are used as a most efficient method to analyze the potentials of junior and senior managers. Advantages of the development centers:
- Real-life observations.
- Observation of performance and behavior.
- Observation of several delegates at the same time (comparison).
- Observation by several observers.
- Observation of defined company-specific criteria.
- Mix of varying exercises and tests.

Objectives of the development center in the context of personnel development:
- Systematic identification of junior managers (potentials).
- Identification of potentials for assignments in other departments/ divisions.
- Focused development of junior managers.
- Identification of the diverse potentials of managers.
- Selection of internal and/or external applicants for managerial positions.
- Identification of individual development needs for managers.

Company-specific requirements:
- Requirements can be derived from the manager's job profiles.
- Company values can then be concretized by observation criteria.
- Managers should be involved when job and observation criteria are developed.

Exercises

From the criteria and the values, company-specific and job-related exercises are developed, which reflect leadership/management situations suitable to extract the desired data. Some examples of such exercises are

- In-basket exercises.
- Group discussion.
- Individual task solving and testing.
- Short presentation.
- Simulation.
- Dialogues with other participants.
- Team-building exercises.
- Communication with employee.

Duration and Participants

Participants in the development of the assessment center are either staff with leadership/management potential or external applicants for a management position. Up to 12 participants can be observed in a development center. Depending on the number of participants, the development centers last one to three days. Observing and solving the exercises requires one to two days. Preparation and introduction of the participants, the evaluation, and the feedback require additional time.

Observers

The observers (between three and six—one for each two participants) should come from higher management (about two levels above the participants) and must be excellently trained. Depending on the observers' experience, one or two candidates may be observed. The observers' tasks are:

- Observation of candidates.
- Rating the candidates' performance.
- Estimating a candidate's management potential.
- Giving qualified feedback.

The observers are trained prior to the development center so that they may get acquainted with the individual exercises. They also should get tips and specific instructions regarding observing and describing behavior, observation and evaluation dimensions, and interpreting and evaluating.

Results

After the observer conference, the observer gives feedback to the candidates. Within a month the candidate will receive a written expertise with the results (i.e., as a debit/actual profile with specific suggestions for personal development) See Figures 5.13, 5.14, and 5.15 for more detail.

Figure 5.13
Integration of Development Assessment Centers

1. **Constructing**
   w Defining the goals and the participants
     (PD pool)
   w Describing and defining the requirements
   w Defining of the observation criteria
   w Checking the exercises for suitability

2. **Preparation**
   w Making the first selection and matching the
     participants (PD pool)
   w Selecting observers
   w Making organizational and logistic
     preparations
   w Sending information and invitation to
     participants
   w Training of observers

3. **Realization**
   w Welcoming the participants, explaining
     objectives and format of the center
   w Working through the exercises and manuals
     by the participants
   w Observating the performance and behaviors
     of the participants
   w Evaluating

4. **Feedback and integration into the personnel**
   development
   w Agreeing about the evaluations
   w Writing the expertise
   w Recommending further development
   w Making the final selection
   w Giving feedback about results to participants
   w Agreeing on support and development
     activities
   w Filing the expertise and the agreements
     in the personnel records

Figure 5.14
Concept for Personnel Development

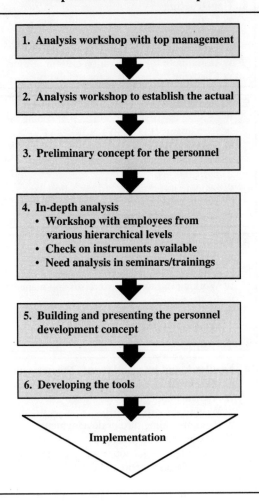

Figure 5.15
Personnel Development through Time

Time Scale for the Implementation of the Personnel Development Activities			
	Quantitative and Qualitative Personnel Planning	**Education and Training**	**Management Development**	**Company Communication**
A. Within 6 months	1. Job requirement profile 2. Evaluation system 3. Analysis of potential	4. Training need analysis 5. Concept of HR development 6. HR development strategy	7. Personnel development for management	8. Statements of top management: • Showcase • Project group
B. Within 12 months	1. Succession planning 2. Career planning	3. Seminars Training Workshops	4. Personnel development - coordinators' meeting 5. Coaching	6. Employee's bulletin
C. Conceptional Within 2 years	1. Job rotation 2. Individual development programs	3. Training on the job 4. Trainee programs	5. Leadership-style analysis	6. Roundtable meetings 7. Employees' experiences
D.	1. Job integration program	2. HR development program	3. Management/ leadership manual	4. Company philosophy

FUTURE TRENDS

Like all concepts, these personnel development ideas can certainly be improved. But hr TEAM International states that companies using this system are experiencing significant improvement in employee performance and productivity. The same need for personnel development exists throughout most Western European countries, and the classic profession that people once learned and held for life no longer exists. A change of *profession* up to two or three times in one's working life has become rather common. Europe herself is changing at a rapid rate. New jobs and professions emerge. Most larger corporations and their consultants are still trying to figure out what a Euro-Manager should look like—someone who acts just as efficiently in London as in Rome, Brest, or Bratislava.

While the cost of labor continuously increases in Europe, only the most flexible, highly skilled in modern technology, multicommunicative, and self-reliant will survive. Corporations, medium- and small-sized companies must identify their potentials and then train these potentials to their highest abilities. (How to offer opportunities to those who will no longer find their future in industry is the urgent task of the politicians.)

The trends are set: Strategic Selling, Global Key Accounting, Multinational Management, Intercultural Personnel Development, Creating Visions, and Developing Multinational Company Philosophies and Values are the topics emerging into the third millennium.

CHAPTER 6

Scotland

John Mullin, Director
Network, Management, Training
and Development Consultants

CURRENT ISSUES

Every year in Scotland the Training Exchange Service, based in Glasgow, organizes a showcase for the latest and best in training and development topics in the Scottish Region. The 1995 event, *Best Practices '95*, featured technology and management training. The selection of management training categories included Supervisory/Management Development, Multi-skilling, Recruitment and Selection, Training of Trainers, Flexible Learning, and Office Practices. Technology categories included Engineering and Electronic Training, Standards and Qualifications, Technology and Training Aids, and Health and Safety Training.

The seminar and workshop topics at this event considered key training initiatives and provided an indication of the current trends for training and development:

- Practical Guide to Benchmarking.
- Design of Effective Team Building.
- Training of Trainers by Open Learning.
- Growing Your Own Leaders.
- Developing Mentoring and Coaching Advisors.
- Improving on-the-Job Management Performance.
- Multimedia Impact in Management and Supervisory Development.
- Establishing a Multimedia Learning Centre/Technologies and Learning.
- Safety Management in the Outdoors.
- Updates on Scottish Vocational Qualifications.

Additionally, current practices of some corporations indicate a bias for training that emphasizes total quality management and continuous improvement, leadership and team building, the role of global influences, and self-paced learning materials to develop managerial competence in staff relations.

Standard Life Assurance Company

Edinburgh, Scotland

Standard Life Assurance Company is one of the largest Life Assurance Companies in the United Kingdom. The company educates approximately 1,000 managers and section leaders in the understanding and use of staff relations policies and procedures. Standard Life developed the training for this initiative based on two fundamental conclusions from their analysis of the audience: (1) conventional classroom teaching of staff relations topics might not be attractive to the target community and (2) related retention and use of information from seminars/workshops might be limited. As a result of this analysis, the company elected to develop individualized, open-learning modules.

Standard Life engaged Network, a management consulting firm in Glasgow, to design, develop, and deliver modules on seven staff relations topics: Grievance, Discipline, Conduct, Company Policy, Capability and Performance, Absence, Redeployment, and Long-Term Absence. In the first phase of the project, Standard Life Staff Relations Advisors reviewed the policies and procedures, cases, and caseload files associated with each of the topics. From these reviews, they produced written overviews, which they gave to Network for compilation into a Distance or Open-Learning Document.

Before the development work began, focus groups of managers and employees met to determine the potential benefits to be gained from a better understanding of staff relations topics and to identify any concerns they had about staff relations. Another objective was to decide which of the seven key topics for training modules were most needed by managers and leaders.

Based on their conclusions, Standard Life and Network were able to identify the best sequence for development of learning modules. The first module chosen for development was *Absence*. To create the approach, they produced draft information about the policies and procedures concerning absence of employees, reviewed the draft material, and developed questions that would enable them to clarify their understanding of the procedures.

Then a learning format was produced that provided opportunities for learners to respond to open and closed questions and multiple-choice options, and the best responses were identified.

At this stage, the learning document was considered to be a draft and ready to be pilot tested. For the first pilot of *Absence*, they selected a group of managers who had attended the focus group meeting and presented them with the draft learning package. As a result of the pilot, one disadvantage of the approach was uncovered very quickly. Because people learn at different paces, it was disruptive to individual concentration when learners in the group asked the training designer questions. Furthermore, some participants finished the package in the time allocated, while others did not. For those who did not finish, arrangements were made for them to complete the learning package at their work area with a training designer in attendance.

After the pilot testing, a review meeting with staff relations advisors was held to improve the material contained in the module. The participants outlined what worked well and what concerns had emerged about the process and/or content of the module.

If participants had difficulty with a passage, it was rewritten, and some adjustments were made to the learning format based on personal observation and feedback. Then the staff relations advisors reviewed the redrafted version of the learning module for accuracy and final testing.

In subsequent modules, only one significant change was made in the process. Those managers who helped in the pilot testing did so on an individual basis with the training designer in attendance. This allowed the designer the opportunity to discuss issues with the objective of improving the finished article.

From the original list of possible modules, *Long-Term Absence* was incorporated into the *Absence* module. The time required to develop and pilot test each module was approximately two months. After the pilot, a finished product was produced in less than three months.

Almost one thousand managers and section leaders have received modules. Recipients have found the program useful not only as a learning experience but also as a way to review aspects of a policy or procedure when a staff relations issue has arisen. Several managers have reported using the modules as a form of departmental training with staff to reinforce sound staff relations processes.

An increasing awareness of the value of individualized, open learning has been gained as a result of this training. This approach also has the potential to be beneficial in other industries such as insurance and banking. As the tempo of business increases, the advantages of self-paced instruction for busy managers may be more and more attractive to organizations.

Motorola Cellular Subscriber Group

Easter Inch, West Lothian, Scotland

Motorola is one of the largest electronics corporations in the world. In Scotland, the company is a leading manufacturer, employing approximately 5,000 workers in its semiconductor operations and cellular facilities.

For many years Motorola has developed effective training strategies to support its business development—such as Manufacturability, Six Steps to Six Sigma Quality, and Benchmarking. Recently, the company produced an exciting and innovative program, *Protecting Our Environment.* Motorola believes the topic of this program—environmental protection—is of such global importance that it requires all its employees worldwide to participate.

The first objective of the course is to increase Motorola employees' general awareness about environmental impacts. To accomplish this objective, participants are asked to identify global and local environmental concerns. Discussion follows to establish potential links between what can happen locally to the environment and how such impacts can have wider and even global consequences.

Many participants share significant insights into environmental issues. Often, attendees indicate that much of their awareness is gained from contact with their children and other young people who seem to be more environmentally aware than were previous generations.

The course includes two other fundamental objectives: to outline Motorola's approach to environmental concerns and to identify and develop solutions to environmental issues on site.

Throughout the workshop several messages are reinforced:
- Environmental problems are interrelated.
- Business and environment go together.

- The best approach to environmental problems is prevention.
- Motorola's responsibility to the environment, as a major employer
- Individuals taking action make a difference.

To develop environmental awareness, participants are encouraged to observe a video, *The Hole Story*. The video examines the growing concern about the depletion of the ozone layer at the stratospheric level, illustrates the characteristics of ground-level ozone, and describes the causes of ozone pollution. The workshop is designed to heighten awareness about protection from ultraviolet rays even in the relatively damp climate of Scotland, and shows how everyone can make a contribution to reducing pollution—for example, by a more considered use of the motor vehicle. Some of the local, national United Kingdom, and wider European concerns over environmental issues are illustrated, and heavy emphasis is placed on the control of waste.

For a large part of the program, the Environment/Safety Manager, who co-facilitates, presents an outline of the impact of legislation. Additionally, participants are asked to identify sources of environmental pressure on the organization. This serves to illustrate how organizations have to respond to pressure from *green groups* or from government regulations—whether local, national, or international. An important point is made that Motorola will endeavor to operate *above compliance* with regard to environmental regulations.

Globally, there are concerns about achieving sustainable environments, the continuing rise in the cost of waste disposal, and the fact that the cost of waste can often be several times that of preventing the waste in the first place. Motorola, like many corporations, believes that by taking this approach to developing environmental awareness, it can improve its operational efficiency by waste reduction and that there can be significant future advantages commercially. Consequently, the latter part of this program concentrates on preventive and improvement actions that can be undertaken within the facility. To achieve this, participants are invited to audit the facility in order to identify where waste either can be or is being generated. This approach is in alignment with Motorola's global continuous improvement approach and is aimed locally at reducing the occurrence of waste and the related costs of handling such waste.

During the audit, participants are invited to identify sources of waste and to consider improvement by:

- Elimination of the waste or the process causing the waste.
- Substitution by alternative means.
- Consideration of reuse and recycling of materials, where appropriate.

Participants are also invited to comment on process maintenance, improvement, and product redesign, if they believe these may have a bearing on waste reduction or elimination.

At the start of the environmental awareness training, no obvious immediate improvement occurred. However, after three months, the following significant gains were achieved:

- An overall reduction in the mass and weighted volume of a particular type of waste associated with the production of electronic goods took place.
- Liquid waste on the site was virtually eliminated, and currently 48 percent of all cardboard is now recycled.

Along with repackaging efforts, these actions have resulted in significant cost savings that ensure the ongoing competitiveness of the company. Additionally, Motorola has set up an *environmental garden* around its site. The *Sunday Times* environmental award for 1995 was presented to Motorola in recognition of the corporation's efforts in this area.

The story is not complete, however. Since the beginning of 1995, both individuals and groups have shown increasing willingness to pursue more and more actions to minimize or reduce waste. This is exactly what the organization hopes for globally and locally.

As a spin-off from this environmental training program, an additional bonus for the Scottish region is the increased care and attention to environmental issues by Motorola employees.

FUTURE TRENDS

As the next millennium approaches for organizations located in the Scottish region, there is an increasing awareness of the position that the electronics industry occupies. Frequently, Scotland is referred to as *Silicon Glen* because of the relatively high concentration of companies working in the electronics industry.

In the last 30 to 40 years, significant development of this industrial sector has occurred, largely through the process of inward investment by global corporations such as Motorola. This process is likely to continue as this region, which was the cradle of the Industrial Revolution, adapts to the requirements of the Information Age. It is possible that the requirements for skilled personnel in the electronics and related sectors will accelerate the need for training. In addition to the key skills of working in the electronics industry, personnel will need to have a deeper understanding of the quality, continuous improvement, and problem-solving techniques that will be required to support the waste reduction and environmental awareness most global companies will bring.

In the next 10 years, there will be a continuing, ongoing requirement to provide business awareness and interpersonal skills training for managers and supervisors in the electronics sector as well as sectors that are more traditional, such as Scotland's important financial industry. In addition to management and supervisory training, the need for training in vocational skills will increase.

In the next 5 to 10 years, many organizations in the Scottish region will experience the need to train more staff to cope with technological change and to use information technology. At the same time, there is a strong indication that the responsibility for personal development is being transferred to the individual worker. Leaner organizations with fewer human resource specialists are likely to accelerate this trend. The smarter organizations will start to develop increased awareness of supply-chain requirements to their customers and suppliers and will learn strategies of continuous improvement.

Organizations in the food, chemical, and whisky industries will undoubtedly continue to be well represented in Scotland and develop improved technological and organizational approaches. The vibrant oil industry of the northeast region of the country should continue to prosper economically over the next decade but may be more visible in its environmental strategies.

Hopefully, the many small businesses that exist in the country can develop an increasingly serious approach to training and development, and those who work in the retail and service sectors will develop enhanced customer service and product awareness skills.

CHAPTER 7

Scandinavia

Susan M. Vonsild, Managing Director
Interlink

CURRENT ISSUES

Scandinavia covers the three countries Norway, Sweden, and Denmark, all of which have a common cultural, language, and historical heritage. Although there are definitely differences among the three countries, people from the one country consider themselves in the same family as their brothers from the two other countries. In general, they understand each other's languages. Each of these countries is quickest to compare itself with the other two countries, and export, in the first instance, goes to one's closest neighbors in Scandinavia where cultural barriers are lowest.

But each country has its special characteristics. While Sweden is the largest of the three with the most industrialized economy comprising a bigger market, Denmark has a special status because it is Scandinavia's bridge to continental Europe. Unlike Sweden and Norway, Denmark most often thinks *south*—that is, toward its larger neighbor, Germany, and to the European Union. That Denmark joined the European Community in 1973, Sweden voted to join in 1994, and Norway voted totally against EU membership in 1994 reflects this view.

The focus of this chapter is on Denmark, with a single industrial example from Sweden. The Danish economy was marked by a major slow-down, even recession, in the 1980s. Maintaining strength of the Danish/Swedish currency was a major challenge, and Sweden had to float its currency in 1993. In the 90s, however, Scandinavia has been marked by an economic upswing and rapid internationalization. Danes, like the Dutch to the south, have traditionally thought international, learning several languages, since Danish is not exactly a major world language. However, the current wave of internationalization requires some deep-seated changes in organizational structures and employee mindsets.

In addition, extremely sharp competition brought on by the opening of the European market and by worldwide technology changes has forced companies to realize that success, if not survival, requires an organizational ability to adapt and to be flexible. It also requires an unprecedented ability to think and act strategically. Old company structures, therefore, are being radically changed. Large groups of employees have been fired and are finding it difficult to get back into the official labor market. Lastly, the opening of the European Market has brought about a wave of deregulation in industries once considered hallowed as state monopolies. In Denmark, this is the case with telecommunications, postal services, train and inter-island ferry transport, and medical services—to name a few.

This brief description sets the scene against which corporate human resource departments are challenged to find a new role. The following examples are taken from interviews with five different companies from five different sectors. ISS, a Danish-headquartered but worldwide-based company in the cleaning service industry (140,000 employees worldwide); Louis Poulsen, a smaller Danish producer of high-profile design lighting fixtures; Novo Nordisk, a worldwide player in the pharmaceutical industry, large in Danish terms but with its 13,000 employees worldwide relatively small in global terms; East Asiatic Company, a Danish trade company with more than a 100-year history around the world, but which has undergone revolutionary changes in the past four years; and the Swedish Telia, which was formerly the sole national telephone carrier but is now facing competition in its own market from 30 international telecommunications companies that have established themselves in Europe's first deregulated telecommunications economy. Sweden is the testbed for what is to come in the next two to three years in all European countries.

If these companies can be considered representative of the current state of developments in the HRD area in Scandinavia, eight main themes emerge:

1. Emphasis on responsibility—understanding what responsibility and accountability are and how these can be fostered among all employees, leaders, those in middle management, and on the floor.

2. The responsibility of leaders not only for company progress (the bottom line) but also for the personal development of their employees. Therefore, the need to develop new roles and skills, such as coaching skills.

3. In larger companies, the regionalization of the HRD function—to support the employee. A complex world with cultural and language differences does not allow for a centralized approach to HRD.

4. Action-learning, and, therefore, a movement away from standardized training programs.

5. Emphasis on building (international) information networks, so that employees can be part of, and take responsibility for, company development.

6. Emphasis on visible corporate strategies (not just something that top management is involved in), on productivity, and on what each employee contributes to the value-adding activity of the company.

7. Emphasis on skills for managing in the global marketplace.

8. Cross-level, cross-function, cross-company, and cross-national HR programs.

Finally, an example is taken from a singular cooperation between the Danish Scout Movement and three large companies as they together try to define responsibility and the conditions that leaders need to create in order for co-workers to be responsible. Responsibility, accountability, and value-driven leadership are seen as the cornerstones of leadership in the future.

ISS

Since 1992, ISS in Denmark has worked with three other Danish service companies (since expanded to six) to develop a training program for senior management based on action-learning. Cooperation on this program originally began with seed money support from the Danish Ministry of

Education, which gave funding to companies to work on specific training projects with public educational institutions.

As described in Figure 7.1, the program with its eight modules was developed on the basis of in-depth analyses of the needs and aims of the four companies. It is jointly offered once a year to senior managers from the participating companies. The seven module themes are:

- The Manager as a Learning Human Being.
- The Manager as Strategist and Business Developer.
- The Manager as Human Resource Developer.
- Pit Stop Mid-term Evaluation.
- The Manager as Marketer.
- The Manager as a Bearer of Culture and a Creator of Results.
- The Manager as Project Mediator.

Figure 7.1
Leadership Program

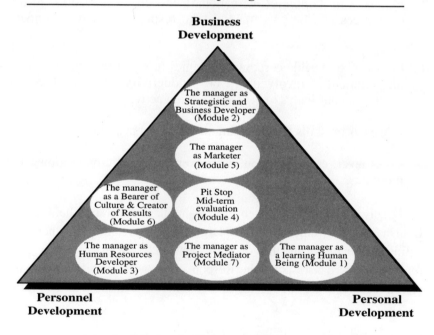

A leadership development program for experienced
managers in the following service industries:
Berendsen Textil Service A/S
Falck Concern
ISS Concern
I. Kruger Concern
PFA Concern
Tele Danmark EDB

The module coordinators and the course instructors are drawn from the four companies, supplemented by external experts when needed. But the most impressive element of the training program is the project work.

During the program, the participants are divided into four-person groups, one person from each company. The groups work throughout the program on a project of interest to the four companies, thereby implementing the theories that are offered to support the project work. A typical project could be "How are the measurements of customer satisfaction in my department?" Considerable time is set aside during the program for this project work.

The immediate superiors of the participating managers function as tutors during the project process. This is an effective way of building coaching skills. In addition, certain employees are trained during the programs to be process facilitators for action learning, skills that can be utilized for other company programs.

The effect of the training program is as follows:

1. Senior managers learn best by doing, and, therefore, the learning is relevant to and tested in their work situations.
2. They implement a project that is chosen because of its potentially positive impact on the participating companies.
3. They build an intercompany network of colleagues at their own level.

The success of this program has been so pronounced for ISS that the action-learning principles have been transferred to training of middle management. At this level the project groups are made up of participants from several ISS subsidiaries, such as the hospital or catering sectors. This has been an important way to build a personal cross-sector network for middle managers across the concern.

Action-learning is also implemented at other levels where new skills must be acquired. A company that has traditionally been quite hierarchically structured, ISS is flattening the organizational structure. One management level has been removed, and a web of teams has been created in the regions (for example, North Jutland, which covers approximately 400 service workers). Each district is responsible for developing its own strategy, and— through a structure of Likkert's overlapping groups in which each team has a representative from a higher level to convey the overall strategy— teams from the supervisory level upward are involved in defining their own strategies. This way, older and younger employees with different educational levels are brought together in teams.

At the level of service workers—for example, in the division dealing with small customers in Denmark and in Finland—work is also planned through teams instead of through top-down instructions. Previously, each worker was assigned a half-day job cleaning for one customer. Now the service workers are divided into groups of three, each team receives a car, and as a team they have the total responsibility for 10 customers. They plan their work and visit all customers within one day. In this way the employees have created more interesting work for themselves, adding an extra benefit of the possibility for full-time employment. This team system started in Scandinavia. England is also beginning to implement a team approach to different contracts, and the vision is that the system will prove itself and spread to other regions and countries.

The team system has created a need for new management skills. The emphasis now is on motivating employees, training, guiding, and teaching them. The key word is *coach*.

While Novo Nordisk believes that less emphasis and fewer resources will be put into training courses in the future and more emphasis will be put into on-the-job training, ISS phrases the shift in other words. They differentiate between company levels.

ISS will still need three types of programs:

- *Vocational training and basic courses* given to new employees who need to learn the basics of cleaning services and specific job requirements (two to three months' programs).

- *Continuing education courses* to meet individual needs—these would be based on individual needs pinpointed during the yearly employee reviews (for example, negotiation skills).

- *Strategic training activities* at a higher organizational level—these would be less standardized than now, would be integrated with the individuals' own plans for their work, and would be evaluated periodically according to established success criteria. An example could be TQM.

The developmental training of senior management in the concern is likely to build on the managers being responsible for presenting best practices at concern-level workshops at Centers of Excellence, participation in transnational task forces, and leadership of local task forces. The training of top managers must be linked to projects that *make a difference* and that support corporate strategy.

In general, for ISS, the longer training programs are typically based on the action-learning principle.

"Ansvar 2000" (Responsibility 2000)

College for Leadership

The Responsibility 2000 program looks in an untraditional way at two aspects of leadership: responsibility and accountability. Since 1994, three large companies—Danfoss (a large manufacturing company), Den Danske Bank, and Rambøll, Hannemann & Højlund (a consulting engineering company); and a voluntary Danish organization (the national Scout Movement)—have worked together to try to define the characteristics of the leaders of the future.

The decade of the 90s is a period of chaos and change on many fronts. In such a turbulent world, the competencies of leaders and employees will be the key to company success. Competency is more than skills, knowledge, and personal contacts. These attributes without strong personal values are insufficient. Values contribute to the individual's *correct* and responsible behavior in each new given situation.

At the same time, the demand for ethics, morals, and personal values as the foundation of management behavior and for the company's role in society will increase. Respect for others' opinions and responsibility for others will characterize the leaders of the future.

Responsibility in society and respect for the individual are significant parts of the philosophy that is the basis for Responsibility 2000. The cross-organization cooperation between industry and the scouts, which seeks to clarify the relation of responsibility and values to leadership, creates insight and renewal for all parties. The companies are gaining a supplement to their training programs with the scout movement's value-based leadership form, and the scouts can use the partners as a mirror to achieve greater self-insight and more contacts in society. Together the partners are defining what responsibility and accountability are and learning how values can thrive in large organizations. This is done through joint analysis and development activities, through joint training programs, and through joint consultancy activity.

The Scout organization builds its work on the fundamental principles of the international scout movement: taking responsibility for the development of one's own ethical views, taking responsibility for one's surroundings and the society, and seeking meaning in life's spiritual dimension. Through a long tradition of volunteerism, the scouts have developed a strong commitment to principles and values and to the spreading of these, so that the leaders in the whole organization—in Denmark alone about 6,000 volunteer leaders—have the same perception of the basic values and work methods of the scouts. Leadership training programs in challenging and active conditions are a central part of this value-transfer.

The three types of activities in the Responsibility 2000 Project are described here in more detail.

1. *Development of concepts*
   Probably the most important part of the joint project is conceptualizing values, the transfer of abstract concepts like values and responsibility, and how to operationalize this transfer. For example, joint groups work on how to describe the fundamental elements of responsibility—what is man's ability to, requirements for, and desire to take on responsibility? What kind of responsibility will a leader have to take in the year 2000? This conceptual work is then operationalized in the joint training programs and consultancy activities.

2. *Training*
   The goal of jointly creating specific training programs and experience-based activities is to create opportunities for participants to develop responsibility and value-based behavior. The training courses are a supplement to what the companies already offer, and they build on the Learning by Doing methods of the scouts.

   One example is a course in responsibility and leadership—developing responsibility and understanding human values as the driving force for human activity. The course looks at responsibility, values, and leadership, and their co-relationships. Participants actively draw experience from the learning process that they are part of. They learn that responsibility is not something that can be given to another, but something that individuals must take upon themselves as employees, as leaders, and as citizens.

Another example is a tool course for better understanding the significance of values and how they can be transmitted with success. A third method is through job training (a kind of "expatriation") of the corporate participants to the scout movement, where they can participate in the leadership courses offered to scout leaders, and where scout leaders are placed in the participating companies.

3. *Consultancy*
   Transferring the knowledge gained through the concept development work to the participating companies is the nucleus of the consultancy activity. Principally, how can values be transmitted, what is responsibility, and what conditions are necessary in order for employees to want to take responsibility for themselves, their company, and their society. The results of the cooperation are also being offered to a broader group of public and private enterprises and institutions.

The work done in this experimental four-party cooperation in Denmark could also become a model for cooperation in other countries between the national scout movement and industry. The Responsibility 2000 group is willing to assist in that start-up process.

Telia

Telia represents what is happening in large companies that are facing radical shifts in their marketplace. Traditionally, Telia has been the main telephone operator in Sweden, owning the telephone cables and offering basic telephone services. But the market has changed. Like the United States before it, Europe will be deregulating the telecommunications industry at the latest by 1998. That means that the national carriers must sell line capacity to anyone who is interested. Since there are low, fixed prices for such access to cables and exchange capacity, the only way that Telia can earn profits is by offering competitive services like cheaper international calls, more telecom activities in countries outside Sweden, and new services based on the IT concept.

In Sweden, unlike all other EU countries, the service market is already totally liberalized. Therefore, a large number of international telecommunications companies are rushing into Sweden and establishing bases in Stockholm in order to carve out a part of this market and—not insignificantly—to learn from the experience of this liberalized market. After 1998, when the service market must be liberalized in all EU countries, these foreign companies will probably move to Paris, Berlin, Frankfurt, or the other large European cities in countries that represent much larger markets than Sweden.

There are more than 30 companies in Stockholm now from such countries as Germany, France, Denmark, the United States, and the United Kingdom. This stiff competition is a preview of what is to come in the other European markets. Therefore, Telia is losing market share in its own territory and being forced to reorganize and to reduce staff.

One major change is that the company is no longer regionally organized with each region—whether north, south, or the Stockholm region—trying to demarcate and maintain its own identity. Telia is now one company taking care of many small, independent companies and employees offering services.

Secondly, Telia is no longer organized according to functions, but is being structured instead according to work *process*. Departments like marketing, sales, and installations have been dismantled. Instead, cross-functional teams have been formed that follow a customer from the first request for services until the customer is satisfied with the services received. Together these two radical changes represent a major challenge for HR programs.

Even Telia's international customers are watching to see how Telia manages these organizational changes.

To be a strong player in the international market, Telia has established Unisource, a strategic alliance with the three national operators in the Netherlands, Switzerland, and Spain. In addition, Unisource cooperates with AT&T in what is known as Uniworld.

This internationalization also requires a new mindset for employees of a company that traditionally, and by the nature of its function, has been inward-looking and Swedish in its ways. Within the Unisource cooperation, economies of scale are to be achieved by some functions from the companies working together—for example, purchasing and R&D. This means that the employees concerned have to learn to cooperate across national boundaries, to understand, appreciate, and work with the systems and methods of four countries.

Secondly, as the company downsizes, an attempt is made to prepare the especially talented employees, for whom a position in the new company may not exist, for assignment to demanding jobs in Telia's international projects.

The program described here—the International Project Management (IPM) program—is designed for persons who will work as project managers in an international environment. The program has been conducted successfully for three years.

The program is modular and covers five weeks of training over a period of six months (see Figure 7.2). The different modules are presented in different locations—for example, the current course is taking place in turn in Kalmar, Sweden; Gothenburg, Sweden; Bristol, England; and Riga, Latvia, with facilitators from different European companies. The course includes Project Management as a certified module given by Chalmers Technical University, Foreign Language Negotiation Skills, Management of Multicultural Projects, Personal Leadership Skills, and Project Finance Administration. The program is demanding and highly interactive. To illustrate, during the group work of the Management of Multicultural Projects program, the participants apply the tools of multicultural project management that are presented during the plenary sessions to real projects that they are working on back home. By the end of the course, the project owners will have received the opinions of 20 other project consultants on how best to manage the cultural complexity of their projects. This is, therefore, yet another example of how action-learning is becoming a preferred training method.

Figure 7.2

Telia's International Project Management Program

Module 1:   Business Administration—understanding the financial conditions of the project.

Module 2:   Writing Reports—communication and report writing in English.

Module 3:   Initiating and Organizing Projects— planning, implementing, terminating, and evaluating projects.

Module 4:   Leadership and Multicultural Aspects— management models and team building in international projects.

Module 5:   Negotiating Internationally—fundamentals of negotiating in a cross-cultural environment.

About 20 participants for the IPM are chosen each time from a pool of candidates put forward by regional managers or by the tele-companies that cooperate with Telia—the Estonian or Swiss telephone companies, for example. The participants have mostly technical education and skills, and sometimes considerable project management experience, but largely from domestic projects.

The first three IPM programs were difficult to sell within Telia because departmental managers were afraid of losing their good people to international projects. Today, however, it is much more obvious—even for tele-employees who have only worked domestically—that attending the IPM is a prerequisite for working internationally and that international project experience is considered necessary for career development. Corporate Personnel even encourages employees to attend the program by offering departments scholarships that cover the course fees.

Departmental managers also have changed their minds. Now they are willing to relinquish their good people because they realize they probably would have lost them anyway with the changes happening in the company. They realize it is better to keep these people in Telia than lose them completely. Also, if they let people go to the program and foreign assignments, they are showing others in the department that their department develops its people. They can thereby *attract* good people. Thus, the IPM program has been one way of promoting job rotation in Telia.

So while Swedtel Academy (the international training arm of Telia) thought that the pool of suitable people for the IPM would probably deplete after some time, the demand is actually increasing. Today the IPM is seen as a natural part of competence building in Telia.

The experience from the IPM and the high demand for it has given impetus to another program that is planned to start up in 1996. It is the IDM—International Development of Managers. Unlike the IPM, which is targeted to project managers, IDM has been developed for experienced Swedish managers who are preparing for future international assignments. It, too, will be highly interactive and built on action-learning.

Novo Nordisk

As a pharmaceutical company, Novo Nordisk is a concern with a high concentration of academically-trained personnel in research and production as well as administration and sales.

A number of initiatives are currently going on in Novo Nordisk at the concern level and are aimed at better linking the corporate vision, mission, and values to performance and effectiveness. The focus is on critical success factors and key performance indicators.

Novo Nordisk has implemented three corporate HR programs that are geared to (1) strengthening employee's personal responsibility for individual professional/personal growth and performance, and (2) strengthening the link between the corporate vision, mission, and values, and the individual employee's behavior. The three programs are built around key competencies, e.g., the qualities individuals personally bring into the job—professionally, attitudinally, and in terms of the roles they play.

The three programs look at different levels :
1. *The Annual Performance Improvement System (APIS)* measures the employees in relation to their immediate superiors and vice versa (the individual level).

2. *Climate Measurements* measure the employees' satisfaction in the group
   to which they belong (the group level).
3. *An Organizational Review or Audit* at the organizational level.

Annual Performance Improvement System (APIS)

The purpose of the Annual Performance Improvement System is threefold:
1. To stimulate the continuous development of a performance-oriented
   culture in the organization.
2. To provide a common language and frame of reference for discussing
   performance.
3. To secure common standards for appraising performance throughout
   the organization.

Clearly stated in the APIS is a list of competencies (see Figure 7.3),
which Novo Nordisk considers critical. These are divided into general
competencies that apply to all employees and a list of leadership
competencies, which are added for individuals with managerial responsibilities.
Each competency is supported by a number of descriptive practices.

Instead of the boss determining what the employee should achieve, the
employee lists individual personal goals in a number of areas. These are
discussed together with the employee's superior. After a year, these goals
and the degree to which they have been achieved are reviewed in a meeting
between the two. After this joint annual review, the completed APIS form
is sent to the superior's boss for information and to the personnel
department. This annual performance improvement review takes place at
all levels in the organization.

The key to APIS is that the employee has the duty of initiative, while
the manager's role is that of coach. This means that if the competencies
are not developed during the year as planned, the employee gets a poorer
grade, since it is an individual responsibility to make sure that the agreed
upon competencies actually are developed. The APIS tool makes it possible
in a visible way to link higher and lower goals, to give two-way feedback,
and to adjust wages to performance realities.

The APIS is proving to be a tool that has legitimized an attitude change—
an attitude that the best people to teach leadership skills to bosses are their
subordinates. Novo Nordisk is making it legitimate for colleagues to teach
each other and to learn from each other. It is not always an easy process
that everyone is picking up without questions. Some people are still afraid
that someone is looking over their shoulders.

Figure 7.3
APIS Competencies

General Competencies

Accountability
- Takes ownership of tasks
- Delivers agreed results on time
- Identifies shortcomings and rectifies these in a timely and systematic way
- Complies with current regulations, policies, procedures, and rules
- Continuously improves professional skills to ensure quality of results

Value Orientation
- Expresses shared priorities and values in daily actions
- Brings problems and questions forward for discussions in the open
- Contributes to lifting the societal and environmental obligations of the company
- Seeks out new inspiration in order to stimulate personal development
- Provides ideas for new initiatives and continued improvements

Team Player
- Builds on the strengths and resolves the weaknesses of working in teams
- Appreciates the value of diverse contributions from colleagues
- Lives up to team agreements
- Stimulates colleagues in order to improve overall team performance and climate
- Appreciates challenges derived from cultural differences

Customer Focus
- Meets changing needs of internal and external customers
- Identifies inappropriate procedures and takes initiative to eliminate these
- Acquires broader business experiences and understanding
- Demonstrates preparedness for a changing environment

Leadership Competencies

Consistency
- Formulates clear targets, ground rules, and deadlines
- Follow up on progress toward targets
- Sets and communicates reasons behind priorities
- Identifies and confronts problems proactively
- Puts corporate perspective first when faced with a managerial dilemma

Personal Integrity
- Acts in a straightforward way that shows a clear link between words and action
- Stays focused under pressure and avoids becoming cynical when times are tough
- Adjusts managerial approach to the situation and the people involved
- Provides timely and useful feedback
- Demonstrates high standards for own performance and social skills

Team Builder
- Communicates common vision in a sharable and motivating way
- Coaches teams to continuous improvement
- Delegates decision-making authority and responsibility
- Shares wins and failures as a team experience
- Uses cross-functional teams as a value-adding factor in strategy implementation

Business Perspective
- Ensures that employees know the customers and their needs
- Translates bigger business perspectives to own unit
- Makes sure that unit's contribution is in line with the corporate vision and strategy
- Draws meaningful conclusions from ambiguities in business environment

Climate Survey

The climate survey was first carried out in 1994/95, the baseline year, and it will be repeated annually. Each person in the department group evaluates 74 statements divided into eight themes and judges them on a one-to-five scale according to two criteria: (1) how important you think this item is, and (2) what you think the actual state is in your group. In effect, the employees evaluate their manager and the manager evaluates co-workers along these key criteria. (Managers are co-workers at the next level where they are involved in evaluating their own superiors.)

The climate survey answers are sent to the personnel department for scoring. Results are discussed among the involved employees sometimes in a seminar and sometimes with a consultant from the personnel department invited as facilitator. By comparing the employees' and the manager's view on the same items, their importance, and actual state, discrepancies become apparent and can be discussed openly. If needed, a plan for extra training or for personal development might be developed for the manager— for example, better delegation skills.

The climate survey is a tool that is also used in the international subsidiaries. It can then reveal some interesting cross-cultural differences in what is considered important and what is judged to be the actual state. When an expatriate is managing a subsidiary, the tool can lead to a fruitful dialogue on the differences that can emerge between an expatriate and the local employees.

Organizational Review and Organizational Audit

The OR/OA takes place primarily at the top management levels. A corporate-level manager is judged on a five-point scale along 10 dimensions that are defined annually by the concern management. These items might be implementation of the climate survey in a department, the fit between business and organization, the degree of employee development, or implementation of APIS and its follow-up. How well a manager does according to these dimensions is the basis for determining his salary development. The OR/OA tool, therefore, helps link salary with performance.

Another key result from introducing these tools has been an appreciation in the organization that the HR area is not something you employ a personnel department to manage. The line managers are beginning to understand and accept that HR is part of their responsibility and function and act accordingly.

East Asiatic Company

East Asiatic Company is one of the most international of all companies in Denmark. Nearly a century ago, the founder H. N. Andersen expressed, "The world is not larger than it can be encompassed by thought."

Against this backdrop, an intriguing story unfolds of how a supertanker can change course in strong winds. In the *old* company, up until the early 1990s, only the company's top management could initiate change. They were, in fact, very well trained through the company route. The usual pattern was that a young person entered the company as a 17-year-old trainee, who was sent overseas to learn the business in one or a series of foreign subsidiaries. After 20 to 30 years, the employee would return to headquarters to a managerial position, and the really top people became board members after their retirement. For over a century, East Asiatic was a company offering life-long employment. The HR function in EAC was one that primarily managed the administration of many expatriations. Personnel manuals grew thicker, as new procedures were noted to take care of each problem as it emerged. Only later did the HR function begin to take a role in personnel development.

The prevailing attitude was that if you were an EAC man, and you had managed a leadership position well in one country, then this experience could be easily transferred to another business unit or another country.

The crisis hit in the early 90s, when bottom-line results showed that economic conditions had changed and that old policies did not fit current conditions. Within a few months a "revolution" took place. Most of the board members were changed, new dynamic top leadership was brought in from the outside, and many of the old key businesses, including the flagship shipping division, had to be sold. Within 10 years from the mid-80s the number of employees plummeted from 39,000 to 12,000 worldwide.

What ensued was a radical change in the leadership style and a turnabout in the company culture. Today the company headquarters has moved to new, light, modern offices from its old buildings with polished brass door handles and exquisite precious tropical wood paneling brought home as a symbol of the trading empire developed over a century around the world. Gone are the old ghosts, most of the old stories and myths, and the old canteens with each individual's own preferred eating place. Now headquarters' employees mix in an open cafeteria with employees of other companies sharing the same office complex.

The new top managers, who were externally recruited and who have academic degrees, have an informal communication style that encourages interaction and focus. They have initiated four activities that have begun to energize the company.

First, since late 1993, a series of strategy courses have been carried out from the corporate headquarters for the "Top 200"—the company leaders from around the world who have been singled out as having particular top managerial potential. The strategy courses were a signal that the engines of development were started up again and that movement would be in a forward direction. Although in the *old* days doing business was mostly a matter of having a *nose* for good deals, the strategy courses get the employees to begin thinking strategically and to understand why strategies are necessary.

Second, emphasis is now on decentralized if not external recruitment. More and more employees are recruited from outside the company in order to match qualifications with the job performance required. Even local nationals are beginning to be recruited to headquarters positions. This would have been unheard of a decade ago.

Third, in 1994/95 the company began to implement career planning. It has started again with the "Top 200" but will reach the lower levels, in turn, as HR skills are developed locally. For example, out of the 500 employees in Thailand, Vietnam, Malaysia, and Singapore, about 20 will now have a career plan that looks at their strong and weak points, their potential and desires, an assessment from their immediate superior, and an assessment of the superior's boss. This process is initiated and managed by the corporate HR office, together with the employees in question and their superiors. The plans are followed up on by the concern level HR office for the senior management and by the local HR unit for the local managers. This whole process is a radical change from the old methods where positions were more filled by the formula "who knows who" than by systematically assessing the match between job profiles and candidate qualifications and skills.

A final method of energizing the organization is the introduction of performance-related pay. While the system has not yet found its final form, it has already focused the employees' attention on what goals they want to achieve in relation to company strategies. Bonus pay is awarded if goals are met before a specific time limit.

The role of the headquarters HR office has developed into participating in the identification and development of key staff wherever they may be in the company and from whatever nationality. Their role has moved from being an administrative body with less emphasis on personnel development to being the mentor of the HR functions at the local levels.

Louis Poulsen

The Louis Poulsen company is a smaller manufacturing company with sales and production subsidiaries in 10 countries with 1,100 employees. A recent shift in management at the divisional level has signaled significant changes in the company, which produces high-profile design lamps and lighting fixtures and sells electric equipment wholesale. The earlier management were excellent traders, always conscious of strict cost management and building up the business on good personal contacts to customers.

The earlier management was focused narrowly on cost management and turnover, whereas the new management also emphasizes other factors that influence corporate success. Approaching corporate leadership with a new kind of professionalism, the new management is also focusing on the corporate vision and mission, establishing an organizational structure that matches the goals, and a market and customer orientation.

They recognize that the HR area is a long-term investment that must accompany the other changes. Three HR areas are receiving attention: the wage system, recruitment, and training and development.

A wage system based on performance rather than seniority is being put in place. Job descriptions with built-in success criteria and yearly employee reviews are making wage differentiation possible.

On the recruitment side, the traditionally strong personnel groups of skilled craftsmen and technicians are being supplemented with more and more people with a higher, if not academic, education. The organizational challenge is to integrate both groups, overcoming eventual skepticism based on a lack of mutual knowledge of the others' professions and building on each other's strengths.

A third area of increased HR activity is training and development. Because of the increasing international competition on the wholesale side of the business, which has traditionally been Danish, major efforts are being invested in the training and development of employees in the wholesale division. It is crucial that they achieve a better understanding of the wholesale market and customers, that they build up strong relations with their customers, and that the purchasing and distribution functions are made still more effective.

For the lighting side of the business, productivity is the nucleus of HR. Emphasis is on employees' understanding of their individual contribution to the value-added sale of a total concept rather than single products, the integration of new technology into the business, and the sale of new services.

The future lies in being a more streamlined, integrated, and efficient organization worldwide with a focused attentiveness to the demands of the international markets.

Information Technology and the HR Function

Three of the interviewed companies pinpointed ways information technology has changed corporate behavior. Novo Nordisk considers itself fairly competent in using IT facilities such as e-mail and video-conferencing (the latter being mostly used among managers and within projects). Concern systems have been put in place across the divisions for personnel and wage administration. The systems work and are used. The next step in the APIS is that each employee's answers will be entered directly into EDB so that the massive movement of paper can be eliminated. Will people use it? Yes, was the answer, if their wages are dependent on it.

In the East Asiatic Company, communication technologies have made the culture shift possible. In the old days a message from an overseas subsidiary in Africa or Asia could take months by boat to reach Europe and the answer just as long in time to return. While waiting for the answer, the person managing an overseas company could continue *reigning* as he wished. As in many companies of the time, memos were rewritten many times before they were sent out of house.

Now e-mail has made communication immediate, informal, and relaxed. Instead of separate finance, economy, and personnel departments coveting their own information, e-mail on everyone's PC—some pressed into using it a little against their wills—has made information flow, report systems, and document transfer immediate and accessible. The speed of information exchange across the concern forces people to react in a different mode than before. There is no longer an excuse for acting independently because information was not available. The increase in amount of information and the technological and organizational means of managing information have perforated the walls of earlier "kingdoms" and strengthened a sense of corporate responsibility.

The way ISS deals with information flow across the concern adds another dimension to how information exchange makes international networks possible.

ISS has central HR values and focus areas, but most HR strategy is decentralized to the subsidiaries where local management knows the local conditions best. The plan is that the persons responsible for HR in the subsidiaries will gather regularly at ISS headquarters in Denmark to exchange experience on practices that work best, to discuss similarities and differences, and to discuss ways that they can support each other.

These HR meetings are organized at the ISS University, located in Denmark at the concern level. Aside from the University's function as training organizer for top level concern management, the University has the responsibility to ensure that best case examples from company subsidiaries around the world are collected, documented, and distributed throughout the company. Two examples are how the ISS service contract at Aabenraa Hospital is managed (hospital sector) and how the service contract at IBM in Austria is organized (industry sector). The written documentation of these best practices may include mode of cooperation with the customer, the service concept used, how the contract is organized and managed, and employee involvement and training. The documentation created is then used in training courses and management development, as well as being distributed to all top managers and departments within the same sector. The object is to collect and spread knowledge and to build up the corporate network.

In the future, subsidiaries that have achieved a particular success may be identified as Centers of Excellence—for example, in relation to service, quality, or job recruitment. ISS University is planning to integrate these Centers of Excellence in its management development with management training workshops organized decentrally at these locations and run by the local management. For the local management, this is learning-by-doing again.

Another way ISS University plans to promote the spreading of corporate knowledge and experience is by building an active database over ISS-internal knowledge of how different services are managed in relation to specific customer segments. That might be a description of a supermarket service concept. Who knows about that field? Who is responsible at that location? By spreading knowledge of who knows what, ISS promotes not only a learning organization but tighter international networks.

Another trend of corporate-level dialogue between the floor and top management—in an international forum—may also be emerging. ISS is the first company in Europe to implement an idea proposed by the European Commission: International Work Councils. The first meeting was held December 5, 1995, and will be followed by yearly meetings between representatives of the service workers in the different European subsidiaries and ISS Group management. The forum is also able to formulate joint projects, such as alternative models for training and development, which could obtain EU funding. This is, in fact, another example of action-learning.

FUTURE TRENDS

Since the interviewed companies, which range in size from 1,100 to 140,000 employees, find themselves in different sectors and at different stages in their history, the views that they expressed about where they see the HR area moving in the future are not identical. Still, a pattern seems to emerge.

1. *Key Competencies*
   Identifying key competencies is pointed out specifically by two of the five companies. In the case of Novo Nordisk, the company has already defined a list of general competencies and a list of specific leadership competencies, each with related behaviors, that it considers to be the foundation of the performance schemes that are being put in place now. In the future, Novo Nordisk will be defining what *processes* are central for the company and assigning a manager to be responsible for the key competencies that are related to each specific process. The vision is that employees will be allocated to shifting competencies. At ISS, one focus of the HR function in the future will be to assist in identifying

key competencies at *all* levels. These then will be the basis of the company HRD programs of the future.

2. *Work Processes*
   A current trend seems to be that organizations will move away from a line organization which is defined by functional areas. Telia is in the middle of implementing such a move to an organization defined by the work *process*. This requires a tremendous mindset shift since the identity of each employee becomes rooted in a new source. Novo Nordisk sees its organization moving more toward a *total project organization,* again defined by processes and competencies. There will be greater independence and more self-managed groups. Telia is implementing cross-functional teams that have full responsibility to follow specific customers from first contact until business is completed to the customer's satisfaction. ISS has been implementing a team approach at the service level throughout Scandinavia and worldwide at the management level. The trend will continue as the organizational method spreads to all regions.

3. *Tightened Productivity*
   Several of the companies mentioned that individual and collective productivity is increasingly in focus as the effects of international competition intensify. Louis Poulsen formulated it well—it is crucial for all employees to understand their individual contribution to the value added. ISS draws attention to the fact that as productivity becomes more and more based on qualitative results, new measurement systems need to be developed that can measure qualitative productivity.

4. *Value-based Leadership*
   The fact that three companies and a voluntary organization have established a formal cooperation and dubbed it Responsibility 2000 in order to delve into what value-based leadership is and how to promote it shows that Scandinavian companies are concerned about linking life's values within the workplace. More and more visions and values will be linked to personal development. As Novo Nordisk formulated it, the future will bring even greater emphasis on the individual's personal responsibility for himself and for the well-being and effectiveness of his group. The challenge will be to hold the spark alive while simultaneously tightening productivity.

5. *Decentralized, Regionalized HR Function*
   Decentralization of the HR functions is increasing in larger companies out of the recognition that the regions know their own conditions best.

For example, Novo Nordisk will regionalize the HRD function to Southeast Asia, the U.S., and Europe. In EAC, the concern level HR function is assisting the regional HR functions to learn skills they can use to take over more of the responsibility for local employee development. As this decentralization and regionalization of the HR function takes place, however, the concern level HR function must take on a new role. ISS suggests this can be accomplished by identifying corporate Centers of Excellence and developing a database of ISS-internal knowledge. This knowledge base will include information on different examples in personnel development programs. How should this be done? How could the division of roles between the regions and the center develop?

Perhaps ISS can provide some direction. By identifying corporate Centers of Excellence and developing a database over ISS-internal knowledge of how different ISS services and customers are managed—and integrating these examples in personnel development programs—the ISS University is strengthening knowledge and information networks throughout the concern. It is taking on a role as information hub and promoter of synergy.

One thing is clear in Scandinavia—whatever the size of the company and whatever the sector, personnel development is recognized as the central element in Human Resource Management. As EAC says, and all the examples reflect, HRD is on its way to being accepted as an integral part of corporate strategy at all levels for which all employees, both managers and subordinates alike, bear a responsibility.

CHAPTER 8

Central and Eastern Europe

Gayle Watson
Director, Consulting Services
The Odenwald Connection, Inc.

Change is the key word for training issues in the Central and Eastern Europe (CEE) region. Tremendous change in the political environment of the region has had significant impact on the economy, business, and workforce. Such change creates confusion for most people not involved in the region on a day-to-day basis. Many countries under former Communist governments have claimed democracy and changed their names. The regional geography map has changed dramatically. Some analysts say the political environment is yet unstable. However, the stage has been set for reform, and continual progress toward establishing a free market in the region can be expected.

Much of the training in the region to date has focused on establishing fundamental knowledge and skills for managers and workers to support the transformation to free market business enterprise. Successful training strategies depend on an understanding of the current political and economic issues as well as the history of each country. Many differences exist between the countries of this region, including the degree of political and economic reform, culture, and history. A great sense of national pride is demonstrated in each of the countries of the region. It would be a mistake to assume that each country is the same in its culture, political and economic environment, labor issues, and educational and training needs.

Europe's Emerging Markets

Countries in the CEE region are often referred to as Europe's emerging markets. As these countries have gained independence from Communist government, they are establishing systems to operate in the free trade market. Many global corporations look to these countries as the *free market frontier* with opportunities to profit from enterprise relationships. Countries in the region offer significant natural and human resources to world markets. Privatization has created the need for new businesses in the region to support the infrastructure required by the free market. As the countries privatize, former state-held interests such as public utilities, telecommunication, transportation, and banks are being sold by governments to private investors.

Key cities in the region are becoming important centers of commerce essential to the opening of trade relations with the world. Hotels in Warsaw, Prague, Budapest, and Moscow are full of international business people attending meetings and conferences related to new business operations in the region. Business journals contain numerous advertisements of global companies entering the market. Articles in these publications are often targeted to educate potential newcomers about investment opportunities and political events that change the business environment daily.

Joining the European Union

As CEE countries continue to emerge as players in the international market, particular countries remain the focus of investment attention from global private and government sectors. Six former Communist bloc countries are targeted to join the European Union: Bulgaria, the Czech Republic, Hungary, Poland, Romania, and Slovakia. These six countries have recently received guidelines from the European Commission to prepare them for membership talks with the European Union in 1997. While still relatively new in the free market, they have made much progress in the past decade. For example, in Poland, the democratic opposition came into power as recently as 1989.

New Independent States (NIS)

More recent to enter the scene of free trade markets are some of the New Independent States (NIS) of the former Soviet Union. The breakup of the Soviet Union in 1991 resulted in independent state governments. While the NIS countries face some of the same issues as other countries in the

CEE, they are in earlier stages of development and therefore have more fundamental needs. At the time of publication, the NIS countries receiving attention include Russia, Ukraine, Kazakhstan, Kyrgyzstan, Moldova, Azerbaijan, Georgia, and Armenia.

The Baltic States

Originally a part of the Soviet Union, the three countries of Estonia, Latvia, and Lithuania are generally referred to as the Baltic states. These countries are usually considered separate from the NIS because they are neighboring states bordering the Baltic Sea and have common economic and trade issues. They are considered more closely aligned with some of the CEE countries than the NIS.

CURRENT ISSUES

Current training issues in this region are directly related to the events surrounding the transformation of former Communist governments to democratic independent states. Three major issues affect progress in the region: political and economic reform, underdeveloped infrastructures, and cultural differences.

Political and Economic Reform

Activity in the region today centers around recovering political stability, regaining external political autonomy, and introducing a market economy. Priorities to accomplishing political and economic reform include the completion of privatization of state-held companies and funding the various projects necessary to support reform. Much of the training in the region is focused on building the capabilities within the countries to make a successful transition to a free market economy.

Privatization

Privatization programs are a key factor in the region for successful transition to a market economy. Privatization programs are usually created by formal government policies of each country in the region. Types of privatization programs vary by country, and the scope of the privatization programs tends to be very broad—aimed at all levels of state-owned enterprises. An important area of privatization is the banking industry. Stability in the banking system and foreign financial investments are key to the economic growth of the region.

Progress in Poland, Hungary, Czech Republic, and the NIS

Generally speaking, much progress has been made for privatization in Poland, Hungary, and the Czech Republic. In 1993, KPMG reported that Poland had given the private sector a 31 percent share of industrial production, 77.7 percent of the construction sector, and 44.4 percent of overall employment. Hungary projected that two-thirds of state-owned assets will have been converted to private property by the end of 1995. Privatized firms seem to be doing well in these countries. The Czech Bank, Zivnostenska Banka, reported a 1994 net profit of 63 percent from the previous year. The Australian Coca-Cola Amatil company has invested about $50 million in the Czech Republic since 1991. It reported 1994 sales were up 15 percent and gross profit up 14 percent from the previous year.

In a few short years since the end of Mr. Gorbachev's presidency in 1991, Russia has developed over 2,500 commercial banks and 600 investment funds. It has privatized 15,779 medium-sized and large companies that produced 62 percent of the official GDP in 1994. Proportionately, Russia's state-owned sector is now smaller than Italy's.

Pace of Privatization and Its Effects

Although progress has been made in privatization, critics say the pace has been slow. A conflict seems to exist about how much control the states are willing to give up. For example, since market reforms began in Poland in 1990, about half of 8,500 state-owned firms privatized or prepared for sale by 1995. However, at the same time, 80 percent of the remaining Polish state assets were concentrated in strategic areas such as energy, oil, transportation, and telecommunications. The sale of such strategic assets are important to generate revenue to support other economic reform programs such as the social security system.

Debates persist about the methods and economic efficiency of privatization programs and practicality of implementation for such programs. Political conflicts about strategies and plans for privatization are often accused for delays in the progress.

Some of the countries face deadlines for privatization, presenting serious concerns about the ability to meet the deadlines and serious consequences. In most cases, meeting privatization goals are an important criteria for integration into the European Union. For example, by the end of 1995, Poland's Ministry of Finance was struggling with plans to meet its bank privatization goals. If the state-owned commercial banks are sold by 1997, the Polish government will be able to tap into a $400 million international fund. At the same time, by 1997, restrictions on foreign banks in Poland will change. Polish banks must prepare for the tough competition. After 1997, it will be much harder to privatize with foreign banks on their turf.

Training Focused on Meeting Privatization Goals

Training has been a very important factor in preparing the various industry segments for privatization. A large foreign investment has been made to provide training for government policy makers and business managers in the region. Training is crucial to enable Europe's emerging markets to meet accelerated privatization goals and position privatized firms to remain competitive in the free market environment. Training is currently focused on economic restructuring, democracy building, and enhancing the quality of life.

Financial Development

Countries in the region have received various forms of financial assistance to accomplish economic reforms. Much of the funding has been designated for educational and training purposes. Loans and investments have been made by foreign government and private sources. Significant sources of financial assistance for training and education in the region are the United States Agency for International Development (USAID) and the UK Government Knowhow Fund.

Economic Progress

Economic progress in the region varies by country, political stability, and reform progress. The economy is showing signs of expansion in the CEE. While inflation figures are decreasing from high numbers of previous years, control of inflation is still seen as a crucial problem. For example, in 1995, the World Bank estimated that Poland's economy grew 5 percent in 1994.

This estimate is consistent with the World Bank report, *Global Economic Prospects and Developing Countries*, projecting that the global growth in trade is expected to rise 5 percent annually in the next 10 years. At the same time, the Polish government revised its 1995 inflation from 17 percent to between 19 percent and 22 percent. *The Wall Street Journal Europe's Central European Economic Review* (CEER) reported 1994 regional inflation forecasts that ranged from 10 percent for the Czech Republic, 19 percent for Hungary, 20 percent for Latvia, 40 percent for Lithuania, 310 percent for Russia, and 810 percent for the Ukraine.

The combined effects of high inflation and the high cost of the social security payments in the region have resulted in an increased cost of wages for employers in Hungary, the Czech Republic, and Poland. Even though the region's workforce is low paid compared to the West, the increased cost of wages has caused some companies in the region to redraw their long-term business plans. Human resource management is becoming more important in the region. Companies are beginning to examine benefits, incentives, and salary programs in relation to workforce productivity.

Underdeveloped Infrastructures

One of the largest obstacles to political and economic reform is the lack of important infrastructures to support the systems necessary to make the transition to a free market economy. Systems targeted for reform include banking, social security, and the legal system. Additional challenges exist in the management of human resources for the new privatized sector.

Banking System

Reform in the banking sector is considered essential to achieve a successful transition to the modern market economy. For example, nearly one-third of the participants in the USAID-funded program, Partners for International Education and Training/World Learning, are in the bank/finance field of study. In the former Communist governments in the region, banks were owned by the state and were limited in their role and function. Therefore, modern banking structures and systems must be established in several areas such as standard accounting and credit practices, banking laws, bank regulation, and examination methods.

Many of the banks are facing the problem of an increasing number of bad loans, a new challenge for CEE banks. Most regional banks do not currently have the technology and operating systems to support modern banking. Lack of up-to-date technology presents a serious concern as Western banks position to compete directly in the CEE market.

Social Security System

Reforms in the social security systems in the region vary significantly by country. Most countries in the region are implementing reform plans that confront the high cost of benefits and deficiencies of the social security systems. In most cases, governments are increasing the employer contribution rates. Some observers say that the reforms in the social security systems are inadequate to meet the future demands of a market economy. In an environment of increasing market competitiveness, consideration is being given by employers to establishing benefit programs that attract skilled labor.

Legal System

The fast pace of change in the region has resulted in outdated laws governing business and personal property. Laws created as long ago as 1930 do not account for business in a capitalist economy. Existing laws are ambiguous and often create difficult and arduous processes for creditors. The lack of a legal infrastructure presents particular obstacles to the development of modern banking system in the region. The banking system is dependent upon well-defined property laws and court resources that allow the perfection of collateral for loans. Banks also need expedient bankruptcy, commercial banking, and accounting liability laws.

Much effort has been made to educate legislators in the region to enable legal system reform. For example, USAID has funded a program for legal development assistance for the CEE in two stages. The first stage is to research and prepare a report about the progress made in the region's bankruptcy laws. The second stage organizes conferences in each of the CEE countries for the purpose of presenting the report to members of parliament, bankruptcy receivers, and government representatives.

Human Resource Management Practices

Managerial Styles

The economic situation created by the Communist governments has resulted in a production-oriented management mindset rather than the customer oriented management viewpoint found in most Western countries. Decades of an emphasis on producing quantity has made customer focus and product quality a secondary goal. Managerial and employee education about quality and the importance of delivering service and products to meet customer expectations is an important priority in the region.

The managerial styles of managers in former Communist organizations are extremely different from the Western style of management. Organizational structures tend to be hierarchical with power concentrated in a few managing directors. Management behavior is control oriented and paternalistic. Information is especially controlled and is shared sparingly. In general, organizational collaboration is not valued. Caution must be given to Western managers who attempt to practice Western management styles. It is unreasonable to expect employees who worked for managers under the previous system to easily change their attitudes and expectations about managers. Management practices, such as open communication and empowerment, are viewed by many old-style managers and employees with skepticism.

Short Supply of Management Talent

The development of managers for the region is an extremely high priority. Most experts suggest that current managers in the region do not possess the needed skills in important managerial competencies including fundamental knowledge of business, organizational management, leadership, employee management, performance management, and communication. Rapid expansion of free enterprise in the region combined with a short supply of management talent has led to a focus on management recruiting and education in the region.

Compensation Practices

Under the former socialist systems, decisions about compensation were centralized. Many decisions about compensation are controlled by labor unions and the central government. Additionally, salaries in most companies are determined and known only by the highest level of management. Often, human resource managers do not know the salaries of employees in the company. Even today, compensation systems based on market pricing, pay for performance, and incentives and bonuses are not familiar to most human resource managers native to the region. Controlling and protective management styles discourage the collaboration needed to participate in industry and market salary surveys.

Western companies that have attempted to implement incentive pay plans and bonuses for production have reported very little success. Experiencing the tremendous changes required in making the transition to a market economy, workers seem more interested in job stability than in receiving incentive pay.

Workforce Competencies

Significant gaps exist between the workforce competencies required to move the region into a competitive free market economy and the skills and knowledge of the existing workforce. Professional skills and knowledge needed to manage modern business operations have not been developed either through the formal educational system or in industry. The need to obtain new competencies is so great, a combination of several solutions will be required including effective employment services, improved recruitment and staffing efforts, and retraining the existing workforce.

Although the workforce is not necessarily trained to perform new jobs created by the free market economy, they are typically well educated. One positive legacy for some of the former Communist governments is universal literacy and an educated population. For example, Russia has one-fourth of the world's trained engineers and has a population well-known for strong mathematical and science abilities. This situation is unique compared to most developing countries. In the case of CEE, the workforce is retraining at a very rapid rate. The educational background enables workers to make the necessary transition into new industries and new jobs. They are very motivated and learn quickly.

Cultural Differences

Ethics

The economic transformation in the region has resulted in mixed opinions about the ethics of government officials and business in general. Some people in the region view privatization efforts with distrust. To them, it is yet unclear how different the new way of doing business is from the old ways. Many people, having lived through various forms of historical oppression, have doubts about the fairness of a market economy and the opportunities available within it. Graft and corruption have been high in the past and remain an area of concern.

Communication

It is important to recognize how cultural differences create communication challenges in the workplace within the region. Vertical hierarchy and controlling management style pervade organizations in the region. Managers and workers are reluctant to engage in cross-functional communication. Employees do not readily participate in open communication behavior. These cultural attitudes about communication are further compounded with a lack of communication infrastructure in organizations. Organizations typically do not have the equipment and technology that provide the communication resources, such as voice mail, fax, electronic mail, and computer-networked workgroups.

Attitudes toward Work

Research about attitudes toward work and the market economy conducted by the Center for Advanced Human Resource Studies (CAHRS) at Cornell University, reveals some important information for Western companies managing operations in the region. Work-related goals such as job security, pay, recognition, and relationship with co-workers and supervisors are important to employees in the region.   Not surprisingly, the younger generation views the market economy more favorably than the older generation and are more open to retraining. In some cases, a lack of understanding exists about the market economy and its benefits for individuals and the country. Uncertainty about the direction of the economic changes and lack of knowledge about those changes result in resistance to change and a tendency to revert to the old behavior patterns.

In the old system of operating, individuals succeeded through relationships with people in positions of power rather than by personal accomplishments. Compliance is usually given to persons in authority to protect personal interests. Therefore, responsibility is often avoided so there will be no consequences. Also, contracts are frequently not trusted.

Personal interactions in business can be summarized as "pretend to cooperate, but seek to your own advantage."

Western companies moving into the region may find it important to help managers and employees of the region understand how their jobs fit into the overall company business plan. Bringing local managers on board with appropriate change management strategies is important to help them overcome the fear of losing their jobs.

Training

Training is clearly a high priority for the region to meet its economic development goals. The focus of training is currently on the transfer of technology, skills, and knowledge. Funds for education and training programs in the region have come from all sources: corporations, Western governments, nonprofit organizations, and universities.

Collaborative programs

Most training and educational programs are collaborative in nature. Partnerships have been created between Western universities and universities in the region to provide formal education to students in the areas of business management and human resource management. Other partnerships provide Western experts teaching regional professionals and managers about particular industry management issues. In most cases, the goal of the educational programs is to establish an ongoing capability for training in the future not dependent on resident Western experts. Following are some of the common elements found in the training programs of the region:

- Establishing links between educational programs and industry.
- Co-development of training materials and programs with regional partners.
- Adapting Western methods within the context of the country.
- Promoting cross-cultural understanding between joint-venture enterprises.
- Developing the capability of local/regional trainers and consultants to ensure continuation of the educational programs.

Examples of a few of these educational programs are described later in this chapter.

Acceptance of Training Provided by Western Experts

Training provided by Western experts has been generally well received by the workers and managers in the region. Interactive training methods used in the West such as group discussion, case studies, and simulations work well, although trainers have to plan carefully for gaining initial group participation since this method is not their norm. The educational model in the region comes from the traditional academic system, where the predominate method of instruction is lecture-based and didactic, with little participation from the participants. The good news about this background is the high credibility automatically invested in the instructor.

Radisson Hotels International

Barbara Weinstein, president of Global Success Strategies, was director of Human Resources for Radisson Hotels International in Poland and Russia and was responsible for directing the human resource and training functions in the opening of the Radisson Hotels in Szczecin, Poland, and Sochi, Russia. She also created a management development program for the local employees of the Radisson Slavjanskaya Hotel in Moscow.

Preopening Training: Customer Service

The goal of preopening training was to ensure that by opening day of the hotel, the local hotel staff of 300 employees were well trained to deliver the Radisson standard of quality customer service. The focus of the training was on job skills and customer service. The training program was eight hours in length, translated into the country languages, and not heavily dependent on written materials. The customer service portion of the program was an adaptation of the Radisson signature customer service program, *Yes I Can*. The program was first implemented in Poland, then later adapted to Russia.

Weinstein spent several months in Poland prior to the opening researching the culture, the workforce, training practices, and customer service standards before developing the preopening training. She utilized the international management team in the hotel, a combination of expatriate managers and local managers, to advise her on appropriate training assumptions and plans.

A first step in her analysis was to determine the customer base. The Szczecin, Poland, hotel was geographically close to Germany. This combined with the fact that the Radisson is a Western hotel company may lead one to assume that the customer has Western service expectations, while guests from Poland and other Eastern European countries may not like the Western style of service. She concluded that the basic principle of customer service— give your guests what they want—applied here. Hotel employees should be prepared to adapt to the range of service expected from their guests.

Weinstein found that it was difficult to ask the local employees to give service in a manner they were not accustomed to. Because Western service standards differed from the host country expectations, the employees were not initially comfortable with the customer service requirements. A key difference in customer service training with Polish employees is the concept and practice of empowerment. In Western companies, the challenge with achieving an empowered customer service staff is providing the resources and support for their decisions. In Poland, Weinstein found the cultural differences make it difficult for an employee to make these decisions.

Weinstein used experiential activities to get the employees involved and comfortable with the new customer service standards. She found several challenges in delivering the customer service training to the Polish staff. One obstacle is the difference in the formal education system in the country. Since making mistakes is not as acceptable as it is in Western countries, participants were initially hesitant to participate for fear of making mistakes. Therefore, it was more difficult to set a climate for learning at the beginning of the classes. Using group tests and competition rather than individual activities seemed more effective.

Most of the training was conducted with interpreters since the native language is important if the participant is expected to learn new ideas. An interpreter may be fluent in the language but not in the topic, so the quality of the translation is important. Preparing the interpreter prior to the training sessions was critical.

An important feature of the training was making the application of class activities and theory to the job. Activities to reinforce skill application included role play in class, on-the-job coaching, and counseling. Follow-up classes with specific situations from the work setting were also conducted. This approach required training, preparation, and coaching of the expatriate managers to understand on-the-job assignments and their role in training.

Management Training

Initially, the Radisson Hotel management staff were brought in for the hotel openings from other hotels internationally. The goal was to hire and develop a host-country management team. Because of the lack of business education in the country, the company took on the challenge of educating the managers in all aspects of business management applicable to the hotel industry. Especially with regard to selecting and training host-country managers, Weinstein cautions Western managers not to impose Western management styles on the local managers. Host-country managers do not have to behave like Western managers to achieve the desired business results. She recommends that Western business managers learn to separate results from strategy and methods when evaluating the operation. Furthermore, it is important to carefully evaluate management practices and policies with the host-country's cultural values and norms to ensure alignment. Otherwise, the employees will not perform as expected.

Key Success Factors

Based on her experience, Weinstein offers the following recommendations to ensure success of training programs in this region:
- Do your homework and investigate. Plan adequate preparation time in the host country. Understand the culture, norms and values, current practice in local companies, and the education system. Create relationships with local resources.
- Be aware of the pitfalls and be flexible.
- Be willing to let go of the idea that we know the best way of doing things.
- Train people how to apply the knowledge learned in the classroom.
- Target all employee communications in multiple languages. Use English only if all employees have fluency, and it is a requirement for the job.
- Arrange for high-quality translation of the materials and in the classroom. Train the staff to understand the material. Avoid literal translations out of context. Review material for a *cultural translation* of the applicability of exercises and examples. Spend time with the translators prior to class. Review the leader's guide to prepare them for the discussion.

Banker Training Programs

The Barents Group manages two USAID contracts to train commercial bankers in the CEE and NIS. The primary goal of the contracts is to establish self-sustaining bank training institutes in specific countries of CEE and the NIS to meet the educational needs of the bankers in the region. The development of a banking institute is focused in three areas:

- Develop the curriculum and deliver the training initially using Western instructors.
- Identify and develop local trainers for the institutes to ensure ongoing continuity of the educational programs.
- Provide technical assistance for the development of the institute. This is accomplished in two ways. First USAID Resident Advisor (RA) consults with the local institute to establish a market presence and develop a curriculum targeted for bankers in their market. Also, the RA identifies the education needs of the institute management staff to develop institute management capability in the areas of marketing, instructional design, and product/service development and pricing.

The overarching goal of the Banker Training Programs is to assist in developing the necessary infrastructure to support the transition of the regional banking industry to operate as a modern banking system in the free market economy and to be competitive on an international scale. Specifically, the institutes are designed to enhance the ability of the banks to perform intermediation, the stimulation of economic growth in the region. Also, the institutes enable the banks to meet international standards of bank safety, soundness, and competitiveness.

The Banker Training Programs are established in the countries in cooperation with the central banks or banker associations. USAID and Barents seek a local partner to co-sponsor the institute. The sponsor's role is to assist the fledgling institute logistically, e.g., providing the facility, marketing, interpreters, and administrative staff for the institute, and to act as a liaison for the institute to the financial sector.

Barents' role is to facilitate the development of the institute and initial management of the training program in the following ways:

- Assess the financial sector for current practices in banking regulation, legislation, and bank supervision.
- Assess the institute strength and weaknesses.
- Assess the individual market bank training needs to determine curriculum and special programs.

CEE Banker Training Program–Comprehensive Trainer Training

Michael Hall has been instrumental in developing and directing the implementation of portions of the CEE Banker Training Program for Barents and USAID. Through the CEE contract, Barents and USAID have established Banking Institutes in five countries in the CEE: The Czech Republic, Poland, Romania, Hungary, and Bulgaria. Hall has managed the on-site programs in Bulgaria and Poland and is currently working on plans for similar institutes in Lithuania.

Hall describes the Trainer Training Program designed for the Bank Institutes as unique and state-of-the-art. His program design combines two important elements for the development of the potential Bank Institute Trainers:

1. **Didactic skills** the development of the participative instructional skills including instructional design, presentation, and case and exercise development.

2. **Technical banking skills** the fundamental knowledge of open-market and modern banking practices. It is important to establish a baseline of technical information and create a context for the understanding of the topical content. The technical skills are learned through a combination of U.S.-based programs and local-based programs. The U.S.-based segment of the program is typically offered in a university setting that provides the necessary learning environment and faculty familiar with the program goals.

He believes that both skill sets are important to develop the level of competency needed by the Bank Institute trainers to transfer the banking knowledge and technology to bankers in their countries.

Polish Trainer Training Program

The trainers are selected based on their banking experience, English language proficiency, willingness to commit to a part-time teaching commitment to the institute for a mutually agreed upon term, and potential as instructors. Over 200 candidates applied for the Polish Bank Institute for 10 trainer positions.

The Polish Trainer Training Program is a full-time program for eight months. The program consists of a combination of classroom training and self-study assignments between the classroom sections of the training. The didactic segment of the training program is conducted in Warsaw for a period of six weeks over four months. Trainees focus on instructional design, presentation skills, and the development of cases and exercises.

Concurrently, the trainees study the technical aspects of banking during the Warsaw-based program consisting of ten weeks of periodic classroom training with self-study reading, exercises and cases for specific banking topics. This segment of the trainer training program is designed to create a broad context as well as knowledge of banking topics.

The Warsaw-based program is followed by a four-week U.S.-based program designed to introduce advanced banking knowledge and concepts and provide exposure to U.S. banking practices. Finally, in Poland the trainer trainees team teach and engage in a practical application of the didactic and technical banking skills.

Lithuanian Trainer Training Program

Hall has modified the Polish Trainer Training Program for Lithuania based on his experience in Poland. Some of the key differences in the Lithuanian program include:
- The institute curriculum and the instructors were developed simultaneously.
- The Lithuanian trainer trainees were part-time participants, not full-time as in Poland.
- The participants were not compensated with salary to be trainers for the institute.
- In general, the technical understanding and English language proficiency of the Lithuanian students was lower than those of Poland.

Three key differences created the need to recruit and select potential trainer trainees differently than for the Poland program. Primarily, potential candidates with the desired banking experience were not as available in Lithuania as in other Eastern European countries. It became necessary to consider candidates for the program with backgrounds other than banking, such a mathematics, statistics, computer science, and physics. Some of the differences in the screening and selection are summarized here:
- Students were tested for language, accounting, credit, and asset liability management.

- A key selection criteria was minimum English language proficiency in the areas of reading and listening skills. These skills were critical for effective participation in the program.

The lack of proficiency in English language and banking experience among the trainer trainee candidates resulted in the following differences in the Trainer Training program.

- A need to change the lecture format in the U.S.-based program. The Lithuanian program incorporated more participation, application exercises to ensure comprehension. Also, the program included more methods to assess the participants' comprehension including level of participation, quizzes, and evaluation of research projects.
- The timing of the U.S.-based program was changed to the first part of the total training program. The program began with 120 hours of English Second Language focused on listening and reading, two key skills to successfully complete the training program. The success of the English language program was confirmed by the fact that posttests reflected significant improvement over the pretests given to new program participants.
- The U.S.-based program includes four weeks of technical training focused on providing the context and technical skills and knowledge of the open-market banking system. The U.S.-based program establishes the foundation for further self-study in Lithuania.
- The Lithuanian-based portion of the program is comprised of six modules of four weeks each: two weeks didactic content and two weeks technical content. Each module is followed by four weeks of self-study in the student's home environment. The final module is a practical application of the didactic and technical skills through team teaching assignments and feedback.

NIS Banker Training Program

The NIS Banker Training Program has established five training institutes since 1993: in Moldova, Ukraine, Kazakhstan, and two institutes in Russia. The NIS project is following the same models established by the institutes in CEE programs described earlier. However, it is in earlier stages of development. Most of the courses are being taught by U.S. instructors in the institutes and throughout the countries based on request. The current focus is on increasing the technical banking knowledge among regional bankers.

Early training topics include core courses in credit, international payment systems, a computer simulation for bank management, foreign exchange, and trade finance. These courses are designed to help NIS bankers deal with the international economy. Later, more advanced banking topics are introduced, such as capital markets, mortgage finance, and customer service. Also, business management topics—such as marketing, human resource management, strategic planning, asset liability, and corporate finance—are offered later.

According to Barents' NIS Banking Course Development Manager Norman Baxter, several factors make training in the NIS different from training in Western countries. First, the NIS students do not often have the same basic understanding of economics as students from Western countries. Also, the NIS political/economic environment is quite unstable as new legislation is passed daily introducing changes in laws and business practices. These changes create constant training challenges, and the issues of nationality are very complex. Unlike CEE countries, the NIS is establishing new nations, and at the same time they are moving to a market economy, they are having to establish national identity. This raises questions such as: *What language will be used for business*?

Generation gaps exist between the new and the older generations. The older generation looks back on the old system as favorable. They knew what to expect in jobs and pay. On the other hand, the younger generation has opportunities they have never had before. They are ambitious and anxious to move forward. Some concerns are being raised about the young people who may leave the country because of the instability.

Based on his experience teaching in the NIS banking institutes, Baxter says trainers cannot make the same assumptions as in the Western classroom. They must be prepared for anything and must expect gaps in knowledge. Students are very sophisticated about some topics and not others. Therefore, training must be aimed at two distinct audiences:
- The very young student, just out of school, with no practical experience.
- The older, more experienced student.

Trainers must be prepared to teach at both levels simultaneously. Most students are curious and eager to learn, and Baxter observes highly intelligent, skilled, and increasingly knowledgeable practitioners in his classes making the transition to banking from engineering, science, and mathematics.

Baxter says that in his experience developing training programs for the NIS, bankers have come quickly up the learning curve. Therefore, the training constantly addresses the needs of a moving target audience. This situation is not typical of other world emerging markets, where educational levels are often lower compared to the NIS. NIS training programs must be designed to adapt to constantly changing needs. One strategy Baxter has used successfully is to plan training in incremental levels.

Key Success Factors

Based on his experience with the CEE Banker Training Program, Michael Hall considers the following points key factors for the success of his programs:

- Effectively assess the country's infrastructure: legislation, regulation, and bank supervision.
- Customize the courses to the needs of the host country. Make sure the case studies and examples illustrate the local situation and embed the concepts and skills presented in the course. Determine how much of the course needs to be *descriptive*—reflective of current conditions in their business environment. *Prescriptive* training applies to the future as the banking system changes. Focus should be placed initially on the *descriptive* training—what the learner can apply most immediately.
- Develop the capability to sustain the training locally. Help the institutes establish a local presence. Teach them to train. Give them the resources to train. Train them to manage the institute at several levels like a competitive training company: administration, curriculum design, marketing, and instruction.
- Prepare for the class with an adequate interpretation, translation, and an open enrollment environment by Western instructors. Select the translator carefully based on familiarity with subject matter.
- Consider all skills required by the participant to successfully implement the skills learned in training. Avoid focusing disproportionately on the technical knowledge. The skills needed for training need to be a mix of technical and management skills. Include companion skills: management, strategic planning, computer systems, human resource management, and organizational development. Most managers in the region are not adequately prepared to fulfill the new demands of the job.

In addition to Hall's observations, Norman Baxter adds the following key factors based on his experience with the NIS programs:
- Establish a local champion to sponsor the program. Identify a sponsor who believes strongly in the program and its purposes—in his case, governor of the central bank, local bankers association, chairman of

the large banks, or a committee member to participate.. Establish a steering committee of government and local industry sector. Make sure those who understand the need for and support the training are on the committee. Work with the committee to determine the training needs, prioritize training needs, review the course outlines, approve the program elements, and promote the institute's products and services.

- Establish ties with local educational programs and universities. Promote interest among potential students entering the industry.
- Research similar programs. Find out the experience, successes, and failures.
- Select the best quality instructors and training materials—get the program off the ground quickly.

Trends for Bank Training

Both Hall and Baxter see much more work ahead for bank training in the region. Training needs will depend on the political environment and the success of the transition to the market economy. If progress continues as expected, the region will need support for building the banking infrastructure and institutional capabilities. Training in business management, human resources, marketing, and planning will be essential. Emphasis on management and operational efficiency will be important in order for the banks to be competitive in the region. They will need skills such as team building, automation, outsourcing, productivity, and developing matrix organizational structures.

Bankers will need training beyond the core banking skills toward more complex topics such as long-term lending, mortgage finance, asset liability management, and asset-based lending. Bankers will need training for mergers and acquisitions, including the organizational and operations aspects of bringing two organizations together. As banking evolves in the region, retail markets will develop. New consumer products will be introduced such as ATM, Point of Sale, and debit cards. Skills such as product development and pricing, sales, sales management, and customer service will become important.

Bank managers in the region will need a greater understanding of global laws and regulations, especially in Europe. As banks move into multinational banking, activity will continue to increase across country boundaries. A rise in European financial industry competition and an increase in the segmentation of the European Union sector can be expected. Activity will increase in non-bank competition such as mutual funds and brokerage operations. Financial institutions will move from core banking skills to a variety of financial products. Europe will evolve into the *universal model* for the financial industry as their laws permit transactions in the financial sector that are currently prohibited by U.S. laws.

Central Europe Human Resource Education Initiative (CEHREI)

The Central Europe Human Resource Education Initiative (CEHREI) at the School of Industrial and Labor Relations (ILR) of Cornell University began in March 1993 with a grant by the Andrew W. Mellon Foundation and was refunded in 1995 for the second phase of work. The Initiative was created to promote awareness and recognition of the usefulness of human resource management and its value to enterprises and organizations in transition and to help establish *centers of excellence* for curriculum development and teaching in human resource management fields in Central Europe through partnerships with area universities. The Faculty of Social Science at Charles University in Prague, Czech Republic, and the Faculty of Management at Comenius University in Bratislava, Slovakia, are ILR's CEHREI project partners. The Initiative planned to accomplish its purpose through the following goals:

- Contribute to the development of a cadre of Czech and Slovak faculty exposed to theory and application of *best practice* in education and training in critical human resource and industrial and labor relations fields.
- Increase the capability of offering courses in the field of human resource management at Charles University in Prague and at Comenius University in Bratislava and to establish country local sites for this education.
- Develop support materials for curriculum and course development and provision.
- Promote awareness of and recognition for the usefulness of human resource management and its value to enterprises and organizations in transition.
- Encourage the expansion of relationships with local resources, enterprises, and government agencies to build support for and enhance the development of institutional and academic goals.
- Develop a base of information about economic transformation and the implications for human resource management.

According to Dr. Linda Gasser, executive director of CEHREI, the program is unique because of its focus on human resource management and its method of building communities of human resource practitioners through collaborative work with faculty in Central European universities and by creating a connection between education and business. The ILR faculty worked together with the Charles and Comenius faculties to design the curriculum, develop course syllabi, observe and co-teach, and share instructional methods. By working together, the project partners developed an understanding of cross-cultural communications, pedagogical practices, familiarity with new global issues, and the opportunity to examine management and industrial development problems with a new perspective. As a result, some faculty have begun new comparative research explorations, and most have developed contacts for future joint work.

During each semester one to three academic courses, such as Introduction to Human Resource Management and Advanced Topics in Human Resource Management, have been co-taught at each partner site with ILR School and partner faculty sharing the load. A management seminar is also offered to managers in Slovakia as part of a continuing education and development effort.

The project has involved nine Central European faculty—two Czech and seven Slovak. More than 30 ILR faculty and staff throughout the school and its extension offices have served as on-site teaching faculty, information sources, seminar leaders, and subject and research advisors. All of the Czech and Slovak faculty have expressed interest in the interactive teaching style used by ILR faculty to stimulate student involvement with the course content—use of film, video, cases, group projects, site visits, guest lecturers, discussion, and computer and role-play simulations.

The program includes summer exchanges to Cornell and site visits to companies in the United States. The program provides the visiting faculty and students with opportunities to meet top-level American managers, observe academic and extension courses, do independent research and course development, have regular consultations with Cornell faculty and staff, and use many venues to observe and relate theory with practice.

During Phase I of the program, a total of 242 students participated in classes in the two countries (the Czech Republic and Slovakia). During Phase II, study exchange opportunities were added for students from ILR, Charles, and Comenius.

A compilation of course syllabi, materials, videos, tests, and texts from courses now exists for use by the Central European universities, and students and faculty continue to develop local cases. The development of local regional business relationships is important to develop course relevance and lay the foundation for future internships for the students, placement opportunities, program support, and project guidance. Companies such as IstroChem, Volkswagen, Slovnaft, Skoda-Plzen, CA-Strakonice, Moser, Borg-Warner, IBM, GET, Pepsico, CEZ, Air Products and Chemicals, Bausch and Lomb, the Washington Post, American Brass, Xerox, Kodak, Canadaigua Wine Company, and Labelon; and trade unions like the U.S. Operating Engineers and the Czech Union of Mine, Oil, and Geology Workers, Union of Chemistry, Union of Hotel Workers, and United Mine Workers, participated with CEHREI students and faculty for class projects and cases analyses.

Overall Lessons Learned

Gasser writes in the CEHREI Phase I Final Report, the program was successful in meeting its initial objectives. She makes several recommendations for the benefit of others using the CEHREI model or creating similar partnerships based on trends observed in the region. These recommendations, which follow, apply to all types of training programs:
- Have clear commitments from all parties of the partnership at the initial stages for what will be provided and how strong the administrative, monetary, and human resource support will be.
- Know the on-site resources that will be available and commitments made for them; spell these out in writing; have people dedicated to solving administrative and academic problems.
- Be true partners; discuss ideas, procedures, needs, budgets, and remedies together to manage them; do the same with evaluations, reports, and follow-up plans. Understand their constraints and culture.
- Obtain good translation assistance.
- Use local examples and cases, not just Western ones; focus on developing comparisons worldwide, and on developing analytical skills.
- Form an advisory committee early and utilize its expertise throughout the project.
- Involvements in this region should be commitments over the long term.
- Exchanges to the U.S. are an integral part of the faculty/instructor development phase.
- Develop faculty as both teachers and consultants/trainers; these are different skills so focus on both.

- Provide regular feedback on content understanding and teaching ideas and style throughout the development stage.
- Be sure courses are not haphazardly thrown in as a part of electives, but that they are part of a well-thought-out plan of education; focus on developing breadth and depth in courses.
- Encourage the use of knowledgeable local or foreign-based practitioners as guest speakers or for site visits.
- Students, with proper guidance, can be good sources of materials and case development.
- Recognize that there is a culture change in teaching and pedagogical structure that must take place; encourage and assist partners to recognize and address this issue.
- Stick to the nitty-gritty of skill development.
- Plan early to handle all logistical details, because things often go awry.
- Use Embassy and Chamber of Commerce contacts.

Gasser believes that human resource management training will continue to be an important topic in the future of the region. Opportunities exist for more specific training about compensation systems, recruiting and staffing, team development, conflict resolution, cross-cultural issues, and communication. As the region progresses in its transition, managers will need to learn how to participate, make decisions, and empower employees to make decisions.

FUTURE TRENDS

The CEE region will continue to experience political and economic instability in the future. Although there will continue to be political changes, typically nationalistic conservatives and liberals contesting for power, most experts predict continued progress toward economic reform. The younger generation will move quickly toward the future, while the older generation resists change and looks toward the old system for relief from the problems created during the transition.

There will be a continuing emphasis on the development of infrastructures to support modern business practices in the region. Transfer of technology will remain an important priority with investments in new technology and operating systems. Education and training have been and will continue to be important emphases in the region. Some of the key training topics for the next few years follows:

Management Skills

The development of all levels of management skill will continue to be an important priority for the region. A great need exists to increase the qualified management pool. Local business schools have not prepared students in the past to manage businesses in a market economy. Although some progress is being made through collaborative projects with Western universities, the task of bringing managers current with Western management practices is enormous. They need training in all areas of the fundamental business management skills such as strategic planning, competitive analysis, financial management, marketing, operations, productivity, quality, and human resource management.

Technical Competencies

The need for the transfer of Western technology and knowledge of various industries will continue to increase as markets open in the region, calling for more efficient and effective methods for technical and skill training. Because the workforce of the region is generally literate and highly educated, more complicated learning technologies and distance learning can be expected to play an important role in retraining workers.

Cross-Cultural Training

As Western companies enter the region, they are bringing key managers and specialists with them, and a trend of integrated management teams will result. Successful joint ventures and partnership relationships will depend on mutual understanding of cultural differences including history, political background, values, norms, and attitudes toward work. Although workers and managers in the region are eager to learn Western business and management practices, Western styles may not be the most effective means to accomplish work in the region. Western managers must be careful to create involvement of partners in the region and demonstrate a real appreciation for management practices that are applicable to the situation and culture.

Customer Focus and Quality Training

As the free market economy evolves in the region, the development of a service culture will define competition in the market. Since focusing on customer needs is new to their culture, there will be a move toward integrating customer focus in all business operations and interactions.

Human Resource Management Practices

Comprehensive training is needed to establish modern human resource practices in companies within the region. Particularly needed are new are concepts in compensation systems, performance management, recruiting and staffing, and performance appraisal systems.

Interpersonal Skills of Empowerment, Decision Making, and Conflict Resolution

Since these are skills not valued in the old systems, it is important to recognize the extent to which these new skills are needed in all levels of employees. They are important elements in achieving a customer service focus, empowering employees to solve customer problems and make customer service decisions. These skills are also important for managers to be successful and to integrate with Western management teams.

Central and Eastern Europe, including the NIS, will be an exciting area for training and education as the region continues to make the transition from Communism. Government leaders, business managers, and all people are being asked to make changes in the way they think, work, and behave that are beyond anything most Westerners can imagine. The application of change management strategies will be important to establishing successful partnerships with governments, business, and educational institutions in the region.

REGION 3: MIDDLE EAST AND AFRICA

CHAPTER 9

Israel

Joseph Shuchmacher, Director
Corporate Training and OD
Dr. Eva Hagi-Niv and **Dr. Amittai Niv**
Consultants
Teva Pharmaceutical Industries, Ltd.

CURRENT ISSUES

The ever-increasing importance of the human factor in Israel, as in other developed countries, has brought about changes in management thinking—from dealing with *manpower* to developing human resources. The human element becomes an essential, expensive, and mobile factor with constantly growing demands upon it: individuals are required to demonstrate a deeper level of competency in what they do, they must show greater willingness to increase their involvement in problem solving, and they must display more responsibility toward all that occurs around them. Both organizational development and training play a central role in this regard. Indeed, most organizations invest vast resources in presenting ideas and concepts, in the development of skills, and in providing the necessary tools. They teach employee management, inventory control, time management, and projects and data banks management; they also teach sales, capital calculations, word processing, and business plans drafting techniques. And they distribute essential information on business development in Japan or an evaluation of the latest developments in Europe after solving the present crisis.

This extensive investment is accompanied by expectations of significant improvements in the ability and the performance of those participating in these programs. Disappointment is quick to follow. It is a known fact that only a small part of what the worker learns is actually applied in day-to-day reality. This is not only due to the material that tends to be forgotten, but is mainly due to the fundamental difficulty involved in translating knowledge into action. Such courses teach, for example, how to diagnose problematic situations but are not able to change them. Studies may provide an awareness of the need for an overall perspective, while in practice employees remain powerless within the complexity of the organizational setup. Necessary changes often seem to be difficult, complex, and unfeasible, and the subject matter taught in the classroom often differs from the way in which senior managers (who no longer participate in such courses) operate.

General dissatisfaction with the outcome of professional training often leads to repeated attempts of a purely superficial evaluation of the results of such training—by measuring participants' satisfaction (thus legitimizing the *rating* culture in this domain) or by attitude surveys of *before* and *after* (leading to difficulties in proving a causal link between the findings).

The rapid growth of courses and workshops is often accompanied by cynicism, which ascribes training, and those involved in it, to the long list of *doubtful* professions in which the connection between theory and practice is all too vague. The joint challenge for both managers and instructors alike is, thus, in building a training environment that creates an organic link between what is learned in the classroom and what happens on a practical daily basis.

Teva: Israeli Pharmaceutical Company

Teva Pharmaceutical Industries, Ltd., develops, manufactures, and markets branded, generic (off-patent), and branded generic pharmaceutical products. As the largest branded pharmaceutical company in Israel, Teva has successfully used its integrated production, manufacturing, and research capabilities to establish a worldwide pharmaceutical business focusing on the growing demand for generic drugs and the opportunities for proprietary branded products for niche therapeutic categories. The company also manufactures and sells bulk pharmaceutical chemicals, hospital supplies, veterinary products, yeast, and alcohol. Approximately 48 percent of its $ 587.7 million in sales in 1994 were in North America and 14 percent were in Europe and other markets outside Israel.

The company's operations are conducted directly and through subsidiaries in Israel, Europe, and the United States. Teva was incorporated in Israel in 1944 and is the successor to a number of Israeli corporations, the oldest of which was established in 1901. Teva grew through a series of mergers and acquisitions, commencing in the 1960s, which consolidated part of the fragmented pharmaceutical industry in Israel, thereby increasing efficiency and greater production capacity.

Teva's activities in Israel are managed in nine geographic regions, while Teva's international manufacturing and marketing distribution is concentrated mainly in the United States and in several East and West European countries.

Teva operates within the international pharmaceutical market that has undergone rapid structural changes in recent years. Its strength lies in the clear division between its different businesses while its growth potential lies in the synergetic link between them. The company's businesses are many and varied—from the production of yeast to the development of ethical drugs. With 2,700 of the 3,500 employees located in Israel, Teva is dispersed over nine different locations in Israel, three European sites, and one subsidiary company in the United States. While most of the company's senior managers developed within the company, they received their professional education in the framework of different disciplines and thus represent varying management philosophies.

Despite the great internal variety, Teva is persistent in its efforts and ambitions to be an Israeli company operating in an integrated manner. On the one hand, the autonomous business units are placed under heavy pressure to initiate activities so as to realize short-term achievements in the immediate financial quarter, yet on the other hand, these units are also required to create a long-term synergetic effect by close cooperation with each other on certain common issues. The employees are thus accordingly required to achieve short-term goals and at the same time to develop a long-term perspective together with an overall sense of responsibility for the entire network. The development of such capabilities is especially relevant to young people joining the company.

The Passage Program

The *Passage* program is designed for young professionals at Teva working in their first position after having completed their university studies. The program's objective is to provide them with an in-depth quality acquaintance with the complex organization that they have entered and to enable them to operate effectively within it as quickly as possible.

Each year young, educated, enthusiastic professionals join Teva, with high expectations regarding themselves and their professional development. They constitute the potential for future professional or managerial development. Since this is their first professional position after having completed their studies, their attitudes and behavior demonstrate the gap between the theory they learned at the university and the actions they are forced to carry out on a day-to-day basis in the organization. They are trained to apply scientific postulations and professional theories and to break down complex situations into simple questions, and they are well versed in the application of linear analysis of complex phenomena. They believe that

- Precision planning leads to correct implementation.
- Management is a rational process.
- A brilliant report may change the world.
- Formal authority guarantees attention and obedience.

All of these premises are put to the test when these young people are required to reexamine professional paradigms and to take part in interdisciplinary operations in a complex and diffused setup. This stark contrast forces the employees to withdraw into a defined, specific, and reactive activity routine. The tendency is to avoid as far as possible any interdisciplinary conflict. Avoiding such activity exacts a heavy price, positive synergy is badly harmed, and Teva's continued growth as a diverse and decentralized company is impeded.

The *Passage* program was designed to provide solutions to these challenges and calls upon workers to adopt a proactive approach while accepting the aims and values of the larger framework. All of this takes place via a controlled attempt to bridge between studies and daily practice. The first program included 24 engineers, economists, pharmacists, and chemists. The second course took place in 1995 with more than 50 participants. The *Passage* program consists of one-and-a-half-day meetings over an eight-month period. According to the model, effective training requires this optimal blend of components:

- The correct subject matter or themes.
- Appropriate methodology.

- A structure designed to achieve the objectives.
- The demand for measurable results.

The subject matter must reflect the training objectives. In the *Passage* program, the personal development objectives of the participants comprised three axes:

1. Building up an analytical ability to understand complex organizational systems and operate within them, while emphasizing the necessary responsibility, initiative, and effort beyond the formal requirements of the position. This is necessary to enable the employees to fulfill their potential from the outset in the group.
2. Familiarization with the different facets of the Teva group—the strategy, the structure, the processes, and the people throughout the company both vertically and horizontally.
3. Familiarization with the relevant personal skills required for operating within a complex business: self-management, role management, and task management.

Program Content

A central topic was studied to help understand the functioning of a complex business organization. Examples of such topics are organizational complexity, the management of changes, promoting tasks in the short term, role management and design, lateral power and influence across the organization, and organizational learning.

Basic self-management skills were taught along with methods of task delegation within the organization, organizational diagnosis, streamlining, assigning objectives, planning and the implementation of improvement plans, teamwork, time management, awareness, and assertiveness (see Figure 9.1 for program details).

Each session included two guest lectures from senior managers in the group (at the level of the business unit managers), who presented the business over which they were appointed and detailed their professional and managerial philosophy.

The final day of the program, the participants presented their projects before their immediate supervisors, members of the group's senior management, the president, and a representative of the Board of Directors. The company president expressed his appreciation of their contribution and presented his vision of the company's future while specifying the place of participants in that vision.

Figure 9.1
The Passage Program 1995: Principal Topics

Meeting Number	I	II	III	IV	V	VI
The Conceptual Part	The organization as a complex system: Diagnosis as a management tool	The management of change: A useful tool in conducting changes—Streamlining	Job design based on time management	Conflict management in a complex organization: From the individual to the organizational structure	Power and influence in complex organizations: Assertiveness	The team: The basic work set-up
Acquaintence with Teva	1. The Teva strategy: Vision, planning, and ability 2. Teva's technological divisions: From industrial and managerial engineering to information management	1. What is a drug? The registration aspect 2. The chemical business recovery plan: Strategy and implementation	1. The operational division: How to turn a pharmaceutical idea into cash flow 2.What does the company comptroller do when everyone is working?	1. Teva's hospital supply business (Travenol) 2.Developing a new drug: How Copaxon® was developed	1. Developing a new drug: Bringing Copaxon® to the patient 2.Why does Teva need a legal department?	1. Teva's international operations 2.Managing the company's human resources
	Breakthrough project: The personal opportunity and the contribution to the organization	Defining the objective of the breakthrough project	Constructing the "map" for the breakthrough project	The project: Building a plan	The project: How to "move" complex tasks without formal authority	Conclusion: Have we learned about task management complex organizations? What is happening in the organization and what does it do to our personal power?

The demands of the participants' immediate superiors should express their expectations in the organization from the results of the training. It does not suffice for the participants to assure the instructors and the group members that they have *actually learned*; rather, they are already expected, during the course of the program itself, to produce a measurable output that ought to express an improvement in both ability and motivation. Those who are to receive the *improved* trainees at the end of the program—the immediate superiors—must give clear expression to their demands for the new level of conduct and to help the participants in reaching it. In this case the demands originate from the superiors, who had taken an active part in the steering committee. The expectations for personal improvement were defined within the confines of this committee via the defining of concrete targets for improvement within the responsibility of the course participants. The superiors also helped the teams in achieving the goals of the projects that were set accordingly.

The structure. The learning framework—the allocation of time, the delegation of the different roles, and the definition of the working processes—should maximize the chances of success. The ambitious goals of the program—both at the personal and organizational levels—required an enormous combined effort from the participants, managers, and instructors throughout Teva, both vertically and laterally. This effort was manifested in three learning formats. The first was in the form of the study group's plenary sessions held at the central location—for one and a half days, including overnight accommodation, once every three weeks. The second took the form of meetings of the project groups that were carried out for a specific customer within the organization. These groups operated between the meetings of the plenary forum, and they met for monitoring and learning purposes with the program instructors and the manager-customers at the participants' working locations. The steering committee that accompanied the program formed the third learning format. It was made up of Teva business units' human resources managers together with senior line managers, particularly the customers and advisors of the various projects. The lessons derived from the conclusions of the program—especially those relating to the planning and implementation of the projects—were studied, and their significance to Teva as a whole was also examined.

The highlight of the program was the projects developed during the course of *learning* and *action*. The projects were carried out by interdisciplinary teams of four to six members each. Each project was designed to provide a breakthrough in promoting an issue of central importance for Teva. A more detailed account of the projects appears later in the chapter.

Projects and Their Implementation

The topics for the projects were defined and recommended by members of the team and were authorized by a senior group manager who also served as a client and team advisor. The project's success was measured in clear *bottom-line* terms: the team had to prove that it had saved money or had recorded a significant income, beyond that required of each one of the members during the course of their routine work. In addition to the personal challenge of initiative and performance set by the project's goals, the implementation led to a deeper acquaintance with a certain facet of Teva, together with the experience of running a team and lateral interdisciplinary work. As expected, the project topics, and the learning that accompanied their implementation, largely reflected the routine and central issues affecting Teva activity during that period.

Eighteen projects were conducted through the *Passage* program. The following are a few examples.

1. *The shock of complexity*: reciprocal dependency and rapid changes are turning the company into a maelstrom of people, roles, disciplines, cultures, products, and approaches. The ability to implement large-scale plans requires the development of new tools and a new language: not only a rational approach that assumes a great degree of certainty (as is learned at a university) but also life in a whirlpool. The project, which involved developing an algorithm to improve decisions and strategies of the chemicals business, required the development of a new way of thinking for today's desired planning. Another project focused upon upgrading the information infrastructure and the construction of tools to enable the optimal selection of generic products for the Israeli market.

2. *Destroying accepted norms.* Rapid growth requires an increase in the extent and scope of operations previously unknown. The *natural* tendency is to simply add more of the same thing. One project examined methods of revolutionizing the company's entire production system.

A recently employed engineer—under the auspices of the *Passage* program—implemented a project involving sweeping changes in the entire complex system. These changes led to significant savings and an increase in the quality level in this essential domain.

3. *Work through interface.* Activity in the new and innovative fields of the company—mainly the development of new products and markets— requires the crossing of organizational boundaries concurrently with the development of the right concept and language combining efforts and cooperation. It is no coincidence that a significant number of projects were directed toward such interfaces. For example:
   - Establishment of a unit to coordinate development and operations in the generic field.
   - Creation of a system of units to coordinate the marketing and production of over-the-counter products.
   - Development of a computerized order system for local market orders.

The interfaces involved here were between the pharmacists' outlets, the group's production division, and its distribution network. They also improved the link between quality control and the R&D laboratories.

4. *Jump-starting processes.* Most processes in the pharmaceutical industry spread out over long stretches of time. The competitive environment is constantly pressing for the reduced time resources. The difficulty in offering a suitable solution to these pressures is a result of the traditional conception linking speed with reduced quality. Those participants working on projects in this dimension of the company's activity were forced to redefine the challenge: instead of perceiving reality in terms of either/or (time or quality), they looked for creative solutions that would enable them to operate on a basis of "this is possible and so is this, too." Examples of this approach: the construction of a series of clinical tests on the Copaxon® drug in Europe, and a shortcut in the process of registering new generic drugs in Israel.

5. *Learning from actions.* Two of the 16 projects conducted under the program ended with no results. One failed due to a lack of agreement between the different clients as to the objectives and the required output. The second one failed because the principal client—who later on did not allow the team's proposed plan to be put into practice—was ignored. These two projects provided real learning material for those who took part in them by spotlighting these questions:

- What is the significance of correctly defining the objective?
- To what extent is the relevant organizational map a crucial element?
- What is the place of the client in these processes?

Results and Conclusions

A student from the Faculty of Management at Tel Aviv University collected data throughout the program for her M.A. thesis. The statistics indicate that almost all the objectives set by the program were achieved.

- The participants did, in fact, undergo a deep familiarization process with the Teva group—becoming acquainted with the entire complex of all the different sections in the organization. This contact with the organization increased their desire to understand it better, along with reinforcing their identification with its aims and culture.
- The participants' exposure to relevant self-management skills in a complex system improved their functional ability, and the group learning process helped them evaluate their needs and define what they need to learn in the future.
- Not only did they acquire knowledge; they also took part in organizational initiatives and operations that went far beyond the call of their normal duty. The success in crossing over the organizational boundaries of their own unit and in achieving a tangible results developed the participants' sense of self-evaluation on the individual level.
- The promotion of central issues on the company's agenda exposed the participants to complex actions across the length and breadth of a complex organization and provided the legitimization for them to make a contribution in the presence of its top management.

The best possible testimony to the success of the program is provided by some of its graduates who have advanced in their position and in the extent of their responsibility.

On the other hand, it has become apparent (yet again) that every success in solving a problem is accompanied by a new difficulty, as in this paradox. When the threshold of ability and expectations rises, solutions are often required that the organization is not equipped to deal with, at least at the present time. Those individuals who succeeded expect more than ever to receive rapid promotion in the hierarchy, along with improved salaries. This is taking place in a company with a flat organizational structure, where years of intense professional achievement are required as a prerequisite for advancement. They also expect more than ever the challenge of projects and constructive guidance provided by their superiors. However, not all managers and superiors are either capable of providing such training or wish to. The ensuing disappointment actually leads the good employees to leave the organization. How can Teva keep them? The answer lies in continual attention to constant development—not only that of the organization itself, but also that of the workers as well.

FUTURE TRENDS

Israel is fast becoming the focus of activity in a complex network in the new Middle East where the boundaries are being removed one by one. It is no longer an isolated *island*. Giant corporations in the East and West regard it as a center of technological advancement, as a crossroads between East and West, and as an exciting meeting point between petrodollars and hi-tech wizardry. Companies that do not benefit from economies of scale—as is the case with most Israeli companies—are being pushed into a multi-option situation where they must find their own specific niche. The move toward such a niche inevitably means greater specialization and increased categorization between professions and businesses. The concept of categorization calls for attention to be redoubled in strengthening synergetic forces operating across and among organizations, and which enable the combined growth of entire complexes.

The disappearing boundaries also have an influence on the individual. A wealth of inexpensive yet high-level manpower—such as those from the Eastern European countries—is likely to take away large portions of future activity from the hands of the Israeli worker. In a situation where the internal competition for jobs is ever increasing, only the best who can prove that they have something extra to offer in a complex system will be able to survive.

The *Passage* program takes place in a very dynamic reality in which people, organizations, and geopolitics are constantly changing. Against such a background, work across the boundaries at these three levels—as well as the relative importance of personal responsibility and development—takes on a new significance. Teva, a microcosm of this phenomenon, calls for active experience and supports an in-depth learning process.

CHAPTER 10

South Africa

Professor P. A. Grobler and **Mrs. M. Marx**
Department of Business Management,
University of South Africa

CURRENT ISSUES

Since achieving full democracy on April 27, 1994, South Africa is beginning to emerge from its economic isolation. Sanctions are being lifted, foreign investment is starting to flow into the country, and overseas competitors are on their doorstep.

The only way South Africa will be able to compete in these new markets is to provide goods and services that are more appealing to prospective buyers than those offered by other suppliers. Two basic issues are at stake when a buying decision is made, namely, the price and quality of the product or service offered.

It is clear that successful companies not only sell what they make, but also make what their customers want—and they make it faster, of a better quality, and frequently at a lower price. According to Ulrich, Brockband, and Yeung, in their article "HR Competencies in the 1990s" (*Personnel Administrator*, Nov. 1989, 91-103), organizations can reach these goals by developing the following:
- Financial capability to reduce cost to customers.
- Strategic capability to provide customers with product design and service.
- Technological capability to supply customers with innovative products.
- Organizational capability to give customers service, quality, and responsiveness.

169

Thus, as pressures related to international competition intensify, South African companies will be obliged to make rapid organizational and cultural changes, and these can only be effected through their employees. Unless these people are in the right places at the right time with the right skills and the right attitudes, the necessary changes will not come about. The key to the desired result is, therefore, effective training.

Competitiveness in Perspective

In the 1995 World Competitiveness Report (WCR), South Africa has slipped seven positions to 42nd from its 1994 position. There are 48 countries on the list. One explanation is that five new countries—Egypt, Iceland, Israel, Jordan, and Peru (all rated higher than South Africa)—entered the rankings for the first time during 1995. It is important to note that this is the third consecutive year that South Africa's rating has fallen since its inclusion in the report in 1992.

However, there are some niches in which South Africa can still be competitive. For example, in 1995 the country occupied the 19th position for *Infrastructure* and the 20th position for *Finance*. In the *People* area, however, it is placed 48th, and 35th for *Management* (see Figure 10.1 for more details).

Thus, although South Africa shows great potential in some areas, it is held back by major deficiencies in others, such as in the people and management categories. In fact, attempts to create the human capital needed for growth are nothing short of disastrous.

Figure 10.2 shows a more detailed description of liabilities in the people area as measured against the other competing countries.

It is clear that if South Africa wishes not only to survive, but also to prosper, companies will be compelled to develop world-class thinking and start delivering world-class products and services. To assist in this regard, effective training can play a vital role.

South Africa's Training Challenge

The biggest challenge facing the new South Africa is that of rebuilding the economy. This process can only be successful if corporations raise performance and productivity standards through skill enhancement and development. Many studies have reduced the factors for sustainable productivity increases to three aspects:

- Education and training
- Economic restructuring
- Better management practices

Seeing to it that a country's workforce will have the necessary mix and level of knowledge, skills, behaviors, and attitudes is the responsibility of two complementary systems—training and education.

Figure 10.1
World Competitiveness Report 1995:
South Africa's Ranking on Some Factors

Factor	Description of Factor	Overall Ranking of Factor out of 48 Countries	Ranking of Some Sub-components of the Factor out of 48 Countries	
Infrastructure	Extent to which resources and systems are adequate to serve the basic needs of business	19	Transport infrastructure	16
			Technological infrastructure	14
Finance	Performance of capital markets and quality of financial services	20	Cost of capital/ rate of return	36
			Availability of finance	24
			Stock markets	19
			Financial services	15
Science and Technology	Scientific and technological capacity, together with the success of basic and applied research	28	R&D expenditure	24
			R&D personnel	44
			Scientific research	31
			Technology management	27
Management	Extent to which enterprises are managed in an innovative, profitable, and responsible manner	35	Management efficiency	41
			Entrepreneurship	15
			Productivity	37
			Corporate performance	32
International- ization	Extent to which the country participates in international trade and investment flows	43	Trade performance	27
			National protectionism	36
			Partnership with foreign firms	45
			Foreign direct investment inward	43
			Cultural openness	39
People	Availability and qualifications of human resources	48	Population characteristics	48
			Employment	43
			Educational services	47
			Quality of life	41
			Attitude of workforce	46

Source: Adapted from the World Competitiveness Report 1995:274.

However, the new government in South Africa has inherited a training and education system with a number of serious shortcomings. For example:

- There is a lack of adequate planning for future skill requirements.
- The unemployed are inadequately trained.
- Inequality of education has left a highly differentiated system with far greater resources being made available on a per capita basis to white students than to blacks, with the ratio of expenditure in the region of 3:1.
- Although South Africa is among the world's greatest spenders on education (23 percent of the national budget and 7 percent of the GDP), there is huge repetition and waste in the system due to separate education departments for Blacks, Whites, Coloreds, and Asians.
- Personnel costs constitute more than 80 percent of all present education budgets.

Figure 10.2—National Competitiveness Balance Sheet - People Liabilities For South Africa

Criteria	Position out of 48 Countries
Population structure/growth	47
Demographic dependency ratio	43
Life expectancy at birth	45
Labor force	41
Career opportunity for women	43
Equal opportunity regardless of background	48
Availability of skilled labor	48
Availability of competent senior managers	44
Brain drain	47
Employment	46
Unemployment	46
Youth unemployment	44
Adequacy of the educational system	47
Pupil-teacher ratio (1st level)	46
Pupil-teacher ratio (2nd level)	44
Level of compulsory education	48
Computer literacy among employees	46
Economic literacy among population	48
Human development index	40
Population per physician	42
Development of aids	48
Motivation to retrain	43
Worker motivation	48
Major occupation of young people	44
Alcohol and drug abuse	46
Attitude of people towards life	44
Values of the society	47

Source: The World Competitiveness Report 1995:276

In order to succeed in the rebuilding process, it is imperative that the various stakeholders—namely the private sector, the state, and the providers of education—interact to establish the composition of required skilled teams so that tactics can be developed to train the individual team members.

The training and development of previously disadvantaged groups for entry into the job market, as well as their training for progression through managerial ranks, is thus a great challenge facing the new South Africa.

Many companies have already embarked on massive training programs in an attempt to meet these new challenges. However, large sums of money are being wasted on *quick fix* solutions. For example, companies suddenly decide they need to empower their employees or implement an affirmative action program and merely look for a program dealing with this topic.

If South Africa wants to succeed in its new environment, it will have to start by building its competency base on four levels:
- National competencies
- Organizational competencies
- Occupational competencies
- Individual generic competencies

As far as national competencies are concerned, in "Competency Controversy: Which Direction to Follow," *People Dynamics* (13(8):23-26), Meyer sees these as the clusters of competencies that have developed in the economy and that reflect industries and services strategic to the country. Examples here are the Swiss watchmaking industry, the South African mining industry, and the American auto industry. Developing countries like South Africa should identify their key industries and develop the competency clusters by creating the necessary research and development facilities needed to support the industry. Tourism, for example, has been identified as a potential key industry in South Africa. However, it will never realize all its potential as long as training and education continue to be fragmented, unfocused, and undersourced.

Organizational core competencies, on the other hand, can be defined as the combination of individual technologies and production skills that underlie a company's myriad product lines. For example, Sony's core competence was miniaturization, which allowed it to produce video cameras and laptop computers. The ability of an organization to identify its strategically important competencies can assist greatly in the effective allocation of resources and training to support its overall strategy.

The combination of units of learning required for a particular job function or profession can be seen as occupational competencies. These can change over time as the technology or work practices alter and as opportunities for further skill formation arise.

Individual generic competencies are those that are largely inferred from performance in a given situation. However, managerial and leadership qualities, for example, are situational and depend on a number of intangible variables such as an organization's maturity and other members of the team. In addition to these competencies, interest is growing in other types of generic competencies, such as the ability to

- Find, process, and use information.
- Solve complex problems.
- Use technology.

The use of a competency-based approach provides for integrated, flexible, and responsive education and training, and facilitates lifelong learning, the new international trend.

Training Practices

Figure 10.3 provides a number of training statistics of 70 companies representing almost 700,000 employees. The companies that participated in the survey are aware of the importance of enhancing and upgrading their employees' skills since almost 40 percent of their training budgets are allocated for this purpose. The expenditure still amounts to only 2.18 percent of total compensation.

However, a number of companies have made tremendous progress in the training effort and some recently received the National Productivity Institute's awards for 1995 (see Figure 10.4). The success stories of two of these companies, as they appeared in *Productivity SA* (1995: 27-43), are briefly discussed.

Figure 10.3
Training Statistics of South African Companies

1. Number of companies reporting: 70

2. Number of employees: 699,169

3. Total training incidents: 369,215

4. Training incidents by race:

White:	46.9%
Black:	46.5%
Colored:	4.6%
Asian:	2.0%

5. Total training expenditure: R627 790,189*

6. Training expenditure by level:
   (as percentage of total expenditure):

Paterson Band	Percentage
D-F	16%
C	26%
B	39%
A	18%

7. Training expenditure by type:

Training Type	Percentage
Technical/skills upgrade	39.26%
Management	21.00%
Operations	4.92%
Literacy	4.14%
Other	30.68%

8. Training expenditure by source:

Internal:	81.4%
External:	18.6%

9. Average expenditure per training incident: R1 943,00

10. Average expenditure per employee: R1 319,00

11. Training and development expenditure as percentage
    of remuneration: 2.18%

*Currency in South Africa known as Rand - 1 U$ = R3,70

Source: Bowmaker-Falconer & Horwitz (1994:15-20)

Figure 10.4
National Productivity Awards for 1995*

THE SEVEN GOLD CLASS WINNERS ARE:
ABSA Bank
Concor Technicrete
Rent-A Sign
Richards Bay Coal Terminal Company
SA Breweries, Beer Division: Alrode Region
Foshini Distribution Centre, Parow

THE TEN SILVER CLASS WINNERS ARE:
Bevcan, Springs
Dano Textile Industries
HL&H Mining Timber, Klerksdorp
ISCOR, Vanderbijlpark
Neil Muller Construction
Sappi Fine Papers, Enstra Mill
SA Air Force, Directorate Managing Services
Spoornet, Empangeni - Rolling Material
Transvaal Suger
Western Tanning Company

THE SEVEN BRONZE CLASS WINNERS ARE:
Europak
Kendal Power Station
Middelburg Ferrochrome, Low Carbon Plant
Nampak Tissue, Klipriver
NCP
Polifin, Monomers Division, Ethylene Plant
Spoornet Northern Cape and Portnet, Saldanha Harbor

THE NINE WINNERS OF CERTIFICATES OF MERIT ARE:
SA National Defence Force
Directorate Oral Health, SA Medical Service
Transnet, Esselenpark Business Unit
Foodcan, Paarl
Johannesburg Municipality, Central Engineering Workshops
Lacsa
National Razor Blade
Polifin, Carbide Acetylene Plant
SA Mint Company
Spoornet, Natal

*Out of 88 entries, a total of 34 organizations in the private and public sectors
received awards in the various categories of the 1995 National Productivity Awards
competition organized by the National Productivity Institute in 1979.

Source:*Productivity SA* (1995: 27-43)

Richards Bay Coal Terminal

The largest coal export terminal in the world, South Africa's Richards Bay
Coal Terminal Company (RBCT), received a gold award. The company
has achieved outstanding results in the following key performance areas:
- Train turnaround time, which has improved by 35 percent (from 6 hours
  20 minutes to 4 hours 5 minutes).
- Ship loading rate, which has improved by 39 percent (from 2,170 tons
  per hour to 3,009 tons per hour).
- Cost per ton handled, which has been reduced by 15 percent (from
  303.78 cents to 258.99 cents).
- Injury rate, which is down by 35 percent.
- Average annual tons per employee, which has increased 38 percent
  (from 68,800 to 94,900).

RBCT is a private company owned by eight of the major coal mining
companies in South Africa. It exports some 60 million tons of coal per
year and is a major foreign exchange earner. It has a workforce of 530.
The results were achieved on the basis of a number of key factors:
- A strong management focus.
- A committed workforce.
- A high level of technological development.
- Good industrial relations.
- Extensive training and development.

The Free State Roads Department

Improved productivity in maintaining the roads of the Free State (Southern
Division)—one of the nine provinces of South Africa—saved the taxpayer
some R5.5 million and also won the province's public works and roads
department a gold award.

The improvement drive was initiated by the area road engineer. Because
of a more than 50 percent reduction in funds for road maintenance, there
was a real possibility of the roads in this province being downgraded with
a general decline in the road service. The engineer found this unacceptable
and called in a consultant. Keeping the budget limitations in mind, a
productivity and quality improvement program was formulated and all
employees from manager to laborer were put through training courses.
The following issues were addressed:

- Improved methods and technology for patching tarred roads and for repairs to culverts and storm drainage pipes.
- Improved general communication, including regular progress and weekly performance meetings, feedback sessions by foremen and team leaders, and daily planning sessions by team leaders.
- The establishment of output standards.
- Site evaluation.

The results of the training was a 30 percent productivity increase in grading, a unit cost decline of 49 percent in heavy grading, and a unit cost improvement of 36 percent in the clearing of drainage pipes and culverts. The life span of tarred road patchwork was increased by 350 percent to 3.5 years, and an increase of 21 percent in equipment utilization also materialized.

Another success story that needs attention is that of the Iron and Steel Corporation of South Africa (ISCOR),

Iron And Steel Corporation Of South Africa (ISCOR)

ISCOR, Ltd., is a minerals and metals company with its Head Office in Pretoria, South Africa. It is ranked 24th in the world on the basis of metric tons of crude steel output and sixth among industrial companies listed on the Johannesburg Stock Exchange in terms of total assets. It employs 48,131 people. Its operations include steel works and mining (iron ore, coal, dolomite, zinc, and silica stone), and it also has a refractory and a number of shipping offices. Its total turnover for 1994/95 was R11 billion and its earnings per share rose from 19.9 cents to 38.5 cents during the same period.

During the year that ended June 30, 1995, its operations were characterized by

- A strong improvement in financial performance.
- A very successful rights issue.
- Increased internationalization and participation in world trade.
- The restructuring of the group to bring about sustained growth.

Future Challenge

The immediate objectives of ISCOR are to make it a truly global business and to find permanently effective means of managing the cycles of its markets. To date, this strategy has required the reengineering of ISCOR's businesses as well as its funding structure. Equally important, it has involved a paradigm shift from the culture of a production-oriented parastatal to that of a market-driven business with a strong emphasis on

- Entrepreneurial values.
- Service commitment.
- Product and process innovation.
- Prudent cash and asset management.
- Employee empowerment.

The success of attaining these objectives is attributed to the fact that ISCOR's people have accepted the challenges of change.

ISCOR and Its People

ISCOR is already preparing for the recruitment and training of a new generation of employees who will provide the skills required for its further development while, at the same time, aligning the profile of its staff complement more closely with that of South Africa's population. In this regard, an affirmative action policy has been agreed to by the unions. This provides for accelerated training for employees from disadvantaged communities but maintains merit as the principal criterion for selection and promotion.

Since the development of human resources within the company is recognized as strategically important, during the 1994/95 financial year the company invested more than R52 million on

- The evaluation of senior management potential and focused development for succession.
- Adult training and education to ensure a higher basic level of education at all ISCOR centers and to establish a culture of learning.
- The empowerment of supervisory staff through specific training programs.
- The management of diversity in the workplace.

Regarding the successes obtained from the management of diversity actions, an outline of the program follows.

Diversity Training Program

The main aim of the program is to improve the relationships between workers who come from a diverse cultural background through a number of training interventions. The program addresses such issues as the following:

- Importance of knowing co-workers.
- Importance and benefits gained from working as a team.
- Strong similarity that exists regarding the values, needs, and ideals of members of different cultural groups.
- Changing of old perceptions and cultivating new ones regarding other cultural groups.
- Importance of stating one's views strongly and with confidence.
- Benefits of a win-win situation when a conflict occurs in the workplace.
- Good communications with the emphasis on asking questions.

The training methodology promotes understanding, cooperation, and team building activities. The participants are divided into four teams consisting of seven members each—two white employees and five black colleagues. The development of a team spirit and effective team functioning are strongly emphasized. This is achieved by means of different sporting activities such as volleyball and obstacle races. Other methods used in the program include one-on-one discussions, group dynamics, short theoretical lectures, practical exercises, and team building.

The relationships between black and white employees at ISCOR before the implementation of the program were tense. Both formed separate groups and did not mix socially or otherwise.

During the implementation of the training program, however, it became evident that the white employees began showing more respect for their black colleagues, and the black employees began to see their white colleagues as their equals. It is interesting to note that the tension between the groups was clearly noticeable before the 1994 election. After April 27, 1994, when South Africa obtained a full democracy, the interaction between the groups improved dramatically. They are now more positive toward each other and view the training as an opportunity to learn more from each other.

The first diversity training program was launched at ISCOR's Glen Douglas Dolomite mine. This mine was functioning at a loss. Although the mine management were skeptical at first, they soon saw the major benefits of bringing their employees together and requested that all employees at the mine undergo training. The results of the training effort for the mine included improved relations in the workplace and increased profits.

FUTURE TRENDS

In order to rectify the enormous shortage of skilled manpower with the limited budgets available, the new South African government has embarked on a number of innovative and resourceful programs:

1. The merging of different educational departments into one controlling body is nearing completion.
2. The government has drawn up an education policy document indicating its intention to integrate the education and training effort within the country, thus making greater collaboration between training institutions and traditional educational institutions possible.
3. On September 13, 1995, the new South African Qualifications Authority Act went through Parliament. This bill improves the quality of education and training at all levels in the country and relates more closely to the economic growth and national development strategy of South Africa with a number of interesting features.

The bill is designed to give national recognition to learning that takes place after compulsory education to encourage the growth of skills and redress the skills imbalance as well as the values deficit in South Africa. The bill also allows for:

- Progression in terms of learning.
- Portability of qualifications across industry.
- Access by opening the door to those who can prove competency.
- Relevance by being work related.
- Equity in standards of training.

To ensure that the bill actually becomes a reality, the government has called for nominations from interested parties to serve on a body known as the South African Qualifications Authority (SAQA). This Authority will have to ensure that the standard-setting process takes place and also will have to establish the minimum level of achievement through national collaboration with all stakeholders. The establishment of standards will be the function of the National Standards Bodies (NSBs). It is projected that once the standards for a particular industry have been set, the NSBs will be dissolved.

In order to earn SAQA recognition, three requirements need to be met, elements of which are required in varying degrees, depending on the field of study/learning. The requirements are

- Fundamental credits (mathematics, science, language, and numeracy).
- Contextual credits (society, economics, politics, industry).
- Specialization credits (particular to a field of learning).

Once standards have been set, Education and Training Qualification Authorities (ETQAs) will perform quality assurance and ensure, through accreditation and monitoring, that standards are maintained. ETQAs will be permanent, accredited substructures of the SAQA.

The following five areas of responsibility have been identified as the core roles of future ETQAs, namely:

- Standard setting (through feedback or facilitation of NSBs).
- Quality assurance (through accreditation and monitoring).
- Provision of training (few ITBs—Industry Training Boards currently provide training).
- External linkages—with other ITBs.
- Capacity building—in terms of knowledge provision and expertise.

In a nutshell, the bill is an essential means of meeting national needs by expanding education and training opportunities especially to those previously denied access and the provision of human resources to boost the economy.

One of the biggest challenges in this regard is the limited budgets available for this purpose. Besides the efforts of the state already indicated, the private sector has embarked on investing large sums of money in the use of satellite communication for education and training purposes. One such development that has reached an advanced stage, and is working effectively, is that of the ABSA Banking Group. This group is one of the biggest financial institutions in South Africa. Their system, known as Africa Growth Network (AGN), is mainly focused on distance education. In Figure 10.5, a list of the AGN's knowledge market products is indicated. The courses offered have already been accredited by local training and educational institutions as well as internationally by the California State University Dominguez Hills (CSUDH).

Initiatives are also being taken on the educational institution side. One of the largest and oldest distance education universities in the world, the University of South Africa, with approximately 120,000 students, has established a committee that is also investigating greater use of technology in education. Because of its increased access to learning—possibly at a lower cost than conventional methods—distance education seems to be the most obvious route that South Africa will follow in its endeavors to regain global economic competitiveness.

Figure 10.5
Guide to Shopping at the AGN Knowledge Mall

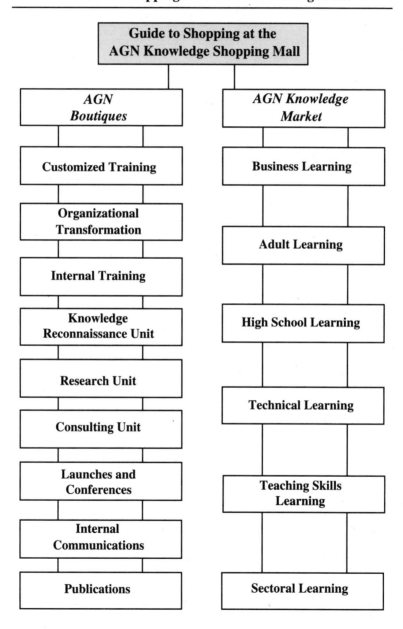

Source: P. Claassen & R. Phillips, Africa Growth Network Information Brochure (1995)

REGION 4: PACIFIC RIM

CHAPTER 11

China

Maura G. Fallon, Managing Director
CSC Management Consulting

CURRENT ISSUES

In late 1978, the People's Republic of China embraced a new strategy for economic development by adopting Deng Xiaoping's *Four Modernizations*: the improvement of industry, agriculture, national defense, and science and technology. By restructuring the management of industrial enterprises using an incremental approach, economic decision making will slowly be decentralized. In seeking to upgrade technology in many sectors of the economy, China is encouraging direct foreign investment. The government is looking to Foreign Invested Enterprises (FIEs) to contribute hard technology transfer, know-how, and practices for managing production and organization. Many U.S. companies see transfer of technology as economically advantageous, especially if the products can be sold, as well as manufactured, locally.

The approach FIEs take to technology transfer depends on the kind of organization that is being set up. The two basic types are cooperative enterprises and joint ventures/wholly owned foreign enterprises. There are a small number of other enterprises.

- Cooperative enterprises or contractual joint ventures where Chinese companies are licensed to use technology are limited projects during a set period. High technology sales contracts of this type often include technical training on the equipment purchased. When the equipment is commissioned, trained local nationals are ready to go to work.

- Equity joint ventures and wholly owned foreign enterprises are of a longer-term commitment. The foreign firm usually contributes technical expertise and advanced equipment along with management expertise. These companies focus on management training, in addition to technical training, of local nationals.

Why is the need for trained managers so great? Under the state-planned economy, factory workers often had limited experience working in plants with modern technology and were unfamiliar with the discipline needed in a market economy. The experience of managers and technicians was in inefficient state-owned enterprises that often had an inflated workforce because of the state's strategy of full employment over profits and efficient use of labor.

Chinese authorities expect foreign-managed firms to play a key role in expediting economic development in China. They also anticipate that these ventures will follow policies that will benefit China, not only the venture of the foreign company. Technical transfer through training and development plays a critical role in this process. Host-national training falls into the areas of technological know-how, functional skills development (accounting and finance, marketing and sales, human resource management, and procurement), managerial skills development, language, and customer relations. One aspect of technical transfer many Foreign Invested Enterprises (FIEs) in China are focusing on is management ideas, processes, and systems. Transforming embedded socialist-economy attitudes toward business and practices in the workplace has come to be one of the biggest issues facing foreign managers in China. At the same time, Chinese and expatriates mention the need to acknowledge Chinese culture and values and to build on its strengths. Ultimately, common ground between the Chinese and foreigners needs to be found so that a third culture, the corporate culture in the joint venture, can be built.

Objectives

Overall objectives of management training programs focus on building company loyalty, aligning employee attitudes with the objectives of the enterprise, and raising employee skills to the level required by FIEs. A lack of prior business skills training in China forces trainers to step back and start thinking from scratch about what trainees already know. Certain concepts that are given in the United States—for example, customer service attitude, and quality assurance—are culturally based. They seem like *common sense* to Americans. Understanding the local culture, and then adapting materials and format to take into account the preferred Chinese learning methods and techniques, is necessary.

Location

Training is being held both in China and overseas. There are advantages and drawbacks to each. The numbers of trainers stationed in China and traveling there from Greater China is slowly growing. Training in China is less expensive and thus is available for a greater number of people in the organization. Training an entire group of people together facilitates acceptance and application of new ideas and methods since China is a collectivist culture, and adhering to group norms is strongly valued.

On the other hand, overseas training and job rotation lets people experience first-hand how to run a business successfully. Seeing how a market economy really works gives employees a concrete model of well-managed enterprises. Working overseas, even for short periods, gives trainees a chance to benchmark and practice new skills and behaviors in a mature organization. They also can prove themselves in a U.S. organization.

Language

A decision must be made on the training language. Some companies train people slated for middle and senior management levels in English because that is the international language of business. Others prefer to train in Chinese as that aids in the assimilation of new knowledge. Technical vocabulary may have to be in English. Still others use bilingual training teams or trainers. Using interpreters may be necessary but requires careful management. However, experience indicates that the quality of interpretation varies vastly. The irony is that the interpreter is doing the training and not the trained facilitator.

Selection

The composition of the training group needs to be examined. The Chinese are accustomed to hierarchy and distance between people at different levels in the vertical structure of organizations. People at subordinate levels may feel uncomfortable verbalizing their opinions, making mistakes, and challenging others in front of superiors. Therefore, separate training programs should focus on different levels of staff. Assess the norms in the local organization, since including people at too many different levels may not provide the best learning environment.

Training Curriculum

Following a survey of American managers in China, the U.S.-China Business Council listed the skills that should be targeted in training programs:

Hard Skills

- Capitalism 101
- Sales and Marketing Training
- English Writing
- Engineering Management
- Computer Skills
- MBA-type Skills

Soft Skills

- Team Building
- General Business
- Total Quality Management
- Time Management and Prioritizing
- People Management
- Communications
- Decision Making and Problem Solving
- Career Development
- Pay-for-Performance, Pay-for-Responsibility
- Trust
- Crisis Management
- Performance Reviews

Steps to Success in Skills Development

Context is important. The initiative is given credibility if those at the strategic apex of the organization are seen to be involved in aspects of the development program, including personally introducing individuals charged with competency development to the participants.

Pretraining and posttraining mentoring are critical to the success of any training venture. This is especially the case in incremental skill building. Individualized coaching and mentoring sessions are needed so trainees can concretely identify how to apply what they have learned.

Training Tips

The following ideas are based on personal experience training in China and discussion with training managers, trainers, and trainees. Trainers are positioned as experts and can establish initial credibility by referring to knowledge and experience. Showing a knowledge of how one's field relates to the situation in China is valued. Training staff can play an important role in getting the operation to run smoothly.

Chinese employees who are participating in management training programs often mention their desire to see local cases and examples used in courses. Course content, case studies, and examples should be based on an understanding of mainland Chinese culture and business environment. This includes the trainees' previous education (probably narrow technical expertise), experience, and daily life situation. For example, most Chinese people cannot drive a car, nor is it likely they will own one. Most have never flown in a plane nor gone abroad. Trainers should not use examples that imply Chinese trainees drive, own cars, or have access to them.

Chinese learning styles must be taken into account. Most Chinese people prefer concrete rather than abstract concepts. Structured training programs are better than those that are loosely designed. Training materials developed for a Chinese audience need to address their specific skill needs, rather than those of an American audience. And the pace of training, particularly if it is in English, may be slower than some foreign trainers are used to.

Extensive written materials are preferred as they can be referred to when people need clarification. Chinese trainees are less likely than Western trainees to embarrass themselves *risking loss of face* by asking questions during the workshop indicating their lack of understanding. Also, workers in China are just now becoming familiar with market economy concepts, such as customer service and quality. The knowledge base is different from that of other countries.

In addition to specific procedures and methods, *soft skills* training should start early on and continue throughout the training initiative. Giving feedback, gathering and sharing information, identifying and solving problems, setting goals and achieving plans, and working as part of a team all fall into this category.

Trainees need to be told why they are learning; telling them what to do is not enough. The reasoning behind Western business practices is not self-evident but is based on years of implicit learning. So, many practices that are culturally bound need to be modified to work in different cultural settings. For example, training methods need to be modified due to different communication styles. Openly managing conflict works in American culture where communication is open and direct. In China, relationships (*guanxi*) are based on harmony, and conflict is usually managed indirectly to preserve face.

Trainers have to understand the expectations of the trainees, especially at the beginning. For example, trainers and teachers are expected to lecture; trainees are expected to be passive. *Learning* is being able to explain what the teacher said. Active training methods and objectives can be successful but are different and need to be explained. For example, action learning and experiential activities can be successful but need to be introduced by explaining the objectives and key learning points. Do not expect explicit feedback from trainees. Read the context and nonverbals.

Since things change rapidly, tolerance for ambiguity is a necessity. This includes being objective enough to modify the workshop in light of participant focus and experience. Present training over a prolonged period of time. Between sessions, participants will have time to digest, accept, and apply what they have learned. In traditional Chinese culture, wisdom is the slow accumulation of experience. Wise ones are expected to reflect on the situation and learn from the past in making decisions. Trainees need time to think through issues and what they have learned before accepting it.

Action steps should be concretely laid out for application on the job. At this point, the role of mentors is critical. Create a safe learning environment both in the training room and on the job so people are not afraid of making mistakes. One trainee said that she had to remember that face is less important than learning. When learning new skills, people make mistakes and lose face; yet through those mistakes they learn. She now focuses on the learning; not on face.

In China, unlike the United States, many materials cannot be borrowed from libraries or purchased. Training materials are virtually unavailable.

It generally takes much longer to accomplish tasks and gather resources than in the United States. Being resourceful and scouting out resources locally and internationally is a necessity.

Retaining Trained Employees

Retention of trained workers is an issue. Extensive training may increase the chance of staff offering their improved skills to other enterprises that offer better compensation or benefits. They may be recruited by outside firms or requested to move by the venture partner or local labor bureau. Some organizations include training bonds or contracts so that trainees will be required to remain in their employ for a certain period of time. Other companies focus on creating a work environment where employees feel satisfied, do meaningful work, and have career development options. Graduation ceremonies and framed certificates are public reinforcement. Knowing that there will be ongoing opportunities for training is a major factor in retention. Astute Chinese managers realize that broader skill competencies are a drawing card that strengthens their career potential and can lead to higher-paying jobs.

Motorola (China) Electronics, Ltd.

Motorola (China) Electronics, Ltd. (MCEL), a wholly foreign-owned entity, is a high-technology firm headquartered in Beijing. It also has manufacturing and sales offices in other cities such as Shanghai, Guangzhou, Tianjia, and Harbin. MCEL's factories manufacture mobile telephones, pagers, semiconductors and other component parts for the domestic and international market. With a leadership role in wireless communications, MCEL has been playing a key role in the rapidly growing telecommunications market in China since 1992. Increasing investment in manufacturing is one of the firm's cornerstone policies to reinforce its position in the Chinese market. Motorola started from ground zero with new manufacturing sites and raw recruits in manufacturing and sales.

A branch of Motorola University was established in Beijing to provide overall training for MCEL staff. MCEL provides training to Chinese technicians on installation, operation, and maintenance of switching technology, base stations, and equipment it sells. Motorola University offerings include skills building in English as a Foreign Language, Communications, Workplace Basics, Customer Service, and Sales. The China Accelerated Management Program (CAMP) of Motorola University sponsored by MCEL was established in October 1994, to supply middle management personnel who can be developed into senior managers in the long term.

Behind the CAMP program is an emphasis on localization of management jobs, which is mentioned as one of the key reasons for the upsurge in management training by many corporations in China. Expectations of the Chinese authorities, the high cost of expatriate employees, and the long-term strategic need for skilled local talent have pushed the drive for localization. Yeo Hiok Khoon, Manager of Strategic Management Programs at Motorola University (M.U.) China, notes that "MCEL wants to send out a message to employees and the government that we are here to stay, we treat China as home, and that localizing management and training managers is part of accomplishing this strategy."

Needs Assessment

CAMP was established because of the great shortage of trained middle managers as noted earlier. Most MCEL employees have worked for the organization for less than three years. Patty Ide, Senior Training Consultant at M.U. China, noted that because of the recent influence of the market economy concept in China, local employees need more management training and development than American managers at the same level. Few managers had any coursework or training background in *soft skills* until recently. As Dave Henrickson, Director of Motorola University–China, often says, "There are no lemonade stands in China." That is, most Chinese have limited experience with sales, customer service, and other soft skills which Americans take for granted.

Objectives

The objective of CAMP is to develop high-potential employees who will become middle managers. Training goals are clearly shared and understood by employees. A CAMP participant validated that by noting that "the Directors and President of MCEL have as their goals to localize jobs."

Selection

CAMP participants are recommended by their business groups, then go through a selection process including interviews and an English proficiency test. Developing strong managers is seen as critical to MCEL's success. Top management, including President P. Y. Lai, are part of the decision-making team that selects participants for the CAMP program. Those who are not chosen for CAMP are assisted in building skills at Motorola University so they will be eligible for future enrollment in CAMP.

This contrasts with the norm in state enterprises where all too often the selection of participants in a training program is seen as a reward or a matter of status rather than one of finding an appropriate match between individual ability and experience, company needs, and the available training.

Curriculum

The CAMP program consists of different phases that develop participants' managerial and personal effectiveness using different kinds of activities:
* Training
* Action learning
* Job rotation
* Teaching others
* Business simulation

Phase 1 involves intensive management training, the study of best practices in specific Motorola operations, and the formulation of individual project plans in which trainees will apply what they have learned.

Phase 2 is focused on planning and implementation of an action learning project, in addition to regular job duties. Coaches and Process Advisors mentor participants during this action learning component. Participants formally present their project results at the end of this phase.

Phase 3 entails job rotation to a Motorola location overseas where participants work closely with other middle managers.

Phase 4 is similar to *Phase 2*, encompassing a more complex Self-Directed learning component. Based on the concept that "You have really learned something when you can teach it," a two-hour training module is developed and presented by participants to the audience of their choice.

Phase 5 is the culmination of the program including the project presentation, an in-depth business simulation exercise, career planning, and a plan for ongoing skills development.

Process Advisors work closely with trainees during the initial phases of the program, enabling application of the skills learned. Time is spent with trainees to ensure that they know why skills training is being offered and what they can gain from it.

Yeo Hiok Khoon expects the curriculum to change over time as the basic skill level of the learners changes and as basic management concepts filter down in the educational system and to the overall workforce. Program design at MCEL is a dynamic process, and the program is constantly being adjusted.

Program Design

The CAMP program design team was an international cooperative venture with some members based at Motorola University in the United States and some in Beijing. CAMP training is presented in English as Motorola feels that future leaders of MCEL need a good command of the international language of business to communicate through e-mail and conference calls, and during job rotations.

Evaluation

There are several process steps to evaluation in CAMP:
- Program participants complete questionnaires after each module.
- Time is spent talking with participants during the selection process and getting feedback from them after every training session.
- Process Advisors sit through every workshop and maintain a close working relationship with trainers.
- Workshops and program elements are modified for greater effectiveness as a result.
- Anecdotal evidence points to the use of skills on the job.
- Plans are under way for a more in-depth survey of skills application.

Retention

Considering the time, energy, and money MCEL expends on employees and a corporate culture that encourages a *family* atmosphere, retention is critical. Motorola has a high retention rate because of training, above-average pay, housing, benefits, and the corporate culture.

Training Trainers

Motorola is building a pool of local workshop instructors to carry on the training initiative. Motorola trains internal employees, scholars at local universities, and others with relevant expertise, to become trainers. Thus far, 50 to 60 people have been certified as trainers in China. The process is strict, including an initial selection process, a five-day basic training skills workshop, co-teaching experience with a master instructor, and a certification process.

FUTURE TRENDS

P. H. See, Chief Representation of MCEL, sees current training efforts as a first step to getting to know the outside world better. The next step is to train Chinese people about working in China. He observes, "Just because they are Chinese doesn't mean they can work in China."

Yeo Hiok Khoon, Manager of Strategic Management Programs at Motorola University–China, sees management training efforts being leveraged to other newly emerging markets, such as India. He observes that recently people and organizations in newly industrialized countries— such as Malaysia, Singapore, Taiwan, and Hong Kong—have given management training a new definition. The trend will grow, with a greater need to train expatriates to operate out of their home environment.

Most training initiatives are weakest in the area of coaching commitment and involvement. Building the skills of expatriates in their role as mentors during on-the-job training is becoming a growing concern in FIEs.

Management training initiatives are still relatively new and will continue to grow. Although many companies are talking about long-term management training in China, few are investing in it. As FIEs mature and make more sustained, long-term commitments to being in China, strategic needs will offset the cost of training.

Chinese enterprises and educational institutions will continue to build a training infrastructure. In time, they may adopt more skill-based programs in addition to the current ones, which are knowledge-based.

CHAPTER 12

Korea

Joel Hastings, Managing Director
K/H Business Communications &
Consulting Co., Ltd.

CURRENT ISSUES

The term *globalization* has received a lot of attention during the past two years. Kim, Young Sam, Korea's first democratically elected civilian president in more than 30 years, built his winning platform on the concept of Sae-gae-hwa or globalization. What does all of this have to do with training and performance trends in Korea? Everything.

What had been previously taboo is now the major theme of advertisements, company slogans, and public service announcements. Companies have been promising to *Globalize by the Year 2000*. In this highly contextual society, managers are being directly ordered to globalize their staff. Budgets have been made and companies seem to be scrambling for the ultimate global training programs. A virtual stampede of new vocabulary is filling the Korean language to help them explain their needs.

Training programs have benefited, too. A program previously called *Business Correspondence* could simply be renamed *Global Communications*, and then sold at a higher price. In fact, many Korean companies pay premium prices for almost any program that promises to increase their *globalization power*. However, after a relatively short time, the energy and pursuit of globalization programs has begun to wane. Many of the early programs failed to deliver what had been promised. Their failure is based on four assumptions:

1. Korean companies are ready to globalize.
2. Korean companies have the necessary facilities and staff in place to administer these programs.
3. Korean companies will be able to internalize and benefit from programs developed for other corporate cultures.
4. The employees have the necessary language skills to benefit from these programs.

All of these assumptions are wrong to varying degrees. Some programs have been successful, but most have failed. Although the major chaebols (conglomerates) have instituted formal policies and practices related to the globalization of their employees, only one seems to be enjoying success.

Samsung

Long before the globalization craze of 1992, Samsung realized that it had to make serious changes in the way it was training its employees. In fact, Samsung has always been a leader in training activities in Korea. During Korea's economic expansion in the 1960s and 1970s, very little attention was given to training at all. Internally, companies relied mainly on traditional Korean customs and manners to develop corporate cultures. Since many Korean chaebols are family owned, they developed more to reflect the personal beliefs and philosophies of their respective chairmen. Employees were usually indoctrinated with these attitudes when they joined the company. Even employee selection was based primarily on what educational institution was attended, what family they belonged to, and what province they came from. Little thought was actually given to the individual. Once they joined the group, they were expected to conform to its norms.

Labor and material costs increased in Korea during the mid- and late 1970s. Korean companies began to look overseas for new markets. Although they had been doing business overseas, it had never been on a very large scale. As their business grew, so did their need to communicate more clearly and effectively in English. Initially, English training was not provided by companies. Employees attended hagwons (language schools) to improve their communication abilities. However, most employees were not satisfied with the training they received. The companies were also not satisfied. It was virtually impossible for them to monitor progress. It was also impossible for companies to hire in-house instructors on the scale that was necessary to meet their needs due to government regulations at the time.

Samsung Corporation, the trading company for the Samsung Group, was the first to feel this acute lack of training. In 1980, Samsung Corporation became the first Korean company to employ an in-house language instructor. In 1982, the company opened the first language training center. Well ahead of its competitors, Samsung set the stage that would continue throughout the 1980s: intensive language study.

By the end of the 1980s, the Samsung Group was beginning to realize that language training was not enough. Other training programs were being developed as well. Samsung looked to Japan for solutions to their growing training needs. This helped Korean companies in two ways. First, it allowed them to see how important facilities were in the training process. Second, they saw the need for implementing the programs they were using. This helped them to create a solid foundation on which they could solve their future training needs.

The Samsung Group Today

The Samsung Group is one of Korea's most successful chaebols. This might surprise some, since Hyundai and The LG Group are better known for specific businesses, but in overall performance and profit, Samsung was ranked higher by the Fortune 500 in 1995. The obvious question one has to ask is, why Samsung?

There are several reasons. First, the leadership: Group Chairman Lee, Kun Hee is unequaled in Korea. His management ideas and policies are truly revolutionary in Korea, and in some cases, Asia. In 1992, Samsung experienced what employees call the *earthquake*. In a matter of weeks, he transformed the policies that he felt were holding the Group back. Furthermore, he made changes that other companies would never have dared to make. He shuffled top management and cut away the deadwood of the Group. He revolutionized not only the shape of the Samsung Group, but in many ways, Korea itself. Although many Korean companies have begun to imitate Samsung's style, they fall short in their commitment to this new management style.

Second, Samsung is strongly committed to globalizing its operations and building a world-class workforce. Like other Korean companies, Samsung is investing heavily in overseas production facilities. But Samsung is also investing heavily in training facilities as well. Samsung knows that in order for these ventures to be successful, it will take more than modern equipment and technology. Training local staff and adapting their cultural attitudes into the overall management process will be a key issue if Samsung is going to succeed. The Group will employ 100,000 people overseas by 2000. To facilitate this growth, Samsung is building a system of eight regional training centers worldwide in strategic areas to help facilitate this process. Plans are also being made for a floating training center that will be able to deliver a wide array of programs to meet the needs of participants in Asia.

Samsung has also started to emphasize self-education. By making workers more accountable in the learning process, Samsung listens to what employees have to say about their training. This type of feedback is very rare in many of the paternalistic chaebols and is one of the reasons Samsung is a leader in the corporate training field in Korea.

This new management style also changed the course of Samsung's training programs as well. The most positive result was the opening of the Samsung Globalization Management Institute (SGMI) in 1994. Samsung built this facility to cultivate the kind of international business professional needed to strengthen their overseas operations and to maximize their corporate competitiveness in the international marketplace.

The goals of SGMI are
- To give the Samsung Group personnel the tools necessary to effectively do business in the new global business environment.
- To put into practice Samsung's corporate philosophy of *Co-existence and Co-prosperity.*

Samsung believes the quality of its people determines its competitive edge. The Group needs people who can speak the local language(s) as well as understand the local customs and etiquette well enough to work comfortably with host-country nationals. These people must also be specialists who can effectively carry out their duties in the global marketplace. Moreover, they have to be able to use information to their competitive advantage and to quickly adapt to changes. In other words, Samsung is strongly committed to creating a world-class workforce.

Currently, SGMI is gathering and processing a wide range of information on specific countries or geographical regions, including data on the overall economy, business practices, individual business areas, and even the personal experiences of Samsung employees in these areas. A full range of information-related services are made available by the institute to support training programs as well as research activities. SGMI's primary mission is to rapidly develop international business people through training and, thereby, contribute to the globalization of the Samsung Group and other smaller companies.

To this aim, SGMI offers a wide range of training programs. Employee confidence in the globalization process is built by training in foreign languages, cross-cultural adaptability, and other important fundamentals. Moreover, training on specific job skills or on individual countries or regions is developing trainees into specialists well equipped for doing international business. The institute is willing to share its know-how by offering globalization training to domestic companies working with the Samsung Group.

SGMI is also creating a very useful database by combining practical overseas business experience with more theoretical research. Information is gathered on local business trends, the status of Samsung's current business and investment activities in the local market, and case studies (both successful and unsuccessful) of attempts to penetrate new local markets. The information is used to support training—programs, consulting services, and research by expatriates and area specialists. SGMI operates Country/ Regional Studies Offices for ten different areas—Japan, China, Russia, Southeast Asia, North America, Central and South America, Western Europe, Eastern Europe, the Middle East, and Africa. The institute also maintains cooperative ties with other specialized research institutes both in Korea and overseas.

The SGMI information network enables the institute to reproduce valuable information. The database can be divided into business-related information and general facts such as local politics, economics, and culture. Data from Samsung operations as well as reports on the personal experiences of Samsung employees (a total workforce of over 190,000) is added to the overall network, as is information from domestic and overseas databases under contract with SGMI. The information is then categorized and analyzed according to type, content, and principal usage. It is then reproduced on the Samsung Group's on-line network (and other systems) as a value-added service.

Samsung's Training System

Each Samsung employee has training on an average of 4.3 times a year. The Group's annual training budget is currently over $100 million and is increased annually. The new 7 a.m. to 4 p.m. work hours have given employees greater opportunities for self-development, and the Group provides various incentives to those who receive qualifications. The main programs operated by Samsung include
- Language Programs
- Key Personnel Training
- Globalization Skills
- Management Development Skills
- Technical Skills

Key personnel training courses are designed to develop core personnel. Programs include the Regional Specialist Course, Techno-MBA Course, Socio-MBA Course, 21st Century Leadership Course, and 21st Century CEO Course. Language programs support efforts in all of these areas and are considered critical for success in these fields.

Language Programs

The importance of language cannot be overlooked where training is concerned in Korea. In 1994, the Korean government estimated that the country spent almost $390 million on English language training. The average Korean businessperson has spent at least 10 years studying English by the time he or she joins a company. Companies, in turn, spend even more time and money making sure their employees have the necessary skills to function in a business environment in either English, Japanese, Chinese, Vietnamese, or Russian. Most corporations use language ability as a criterion for promotion. Samsung, for example, requires employees to be proficient in English and at least one other language before the person reaches a general managerial position.

Language courses are usually broken down in two ways: general language courses and skill-intensive programs. Payment is normally on an hourly basis ranging anywhere from $25 to $130 per hour depending on the experience of the trainers and the reputation of the company they work for. Since the early 1980s, TOEIC has been the standard measurement tool used by most companies to evaluate employee proficiency in English. In most cases, this is the only information companies record about employee language proficiency. This has recently led to problems as many Korean companies are expanding overseas and discovering that even with an 800 on the TOEIC, overseas managers are having trouble communicating and functioning in other cultures. More specifically, Korean companies have noticed the effect on the bottom line. According to Philip Merry, a cross-cultural management consultant, a failed assignment can cost a company more than $200,000.

While some companies are struggling with their language programs, Samsung has made a solid commitment to ensure their programs are well-suited for their employees. Language courses are offered at Group and company level. Samsung has two buildings in the Seoul area dedicated solely to language study as well as four language training centers in the rest of Korea. The group employs 35 full-time language instructors as well as an estimated 200 part-time instructors. Courses offered include English, Japanese, Chinese, Russian, German, French, and Spanish.

Rather than use off-the-shelf programs, the Group tends to develop its own customized language programs. This allows trainers, as well as employees, to focus more on specific problems they are having rather than to take the generic approach that is often too time consuming and redundant.

Language programs at Samsung are constantly being adjusted to reflect the needs of its personnel. As mentioned earlier, Samsung was the leader in language programs, and remains so today. One very good example is Samsung's overseas regional specialist program.

Nemawashi is a word used by Japanese gardeners and businessmen, literally meaning to prepare the soil. Samsung's overseas regional specialist program, begun in 1990, is an excellent example of this theory put into practice. It is part of a *globalization through localization* strategy. The idea is simple yet revolutionary. Knowing that Samsung's future depends on its ability to survive and expand its operations overseas, the Group chooses young employees and sends them to strategic business areas to live, study, and learn on their own. They receive training in the local language and gain direct experience in the local culture. It is designed to develop business people with an internationalized perspective who can deal with the business realities of the next century. For one year, they are given no corporate responsibilities. Trainees overcome cross-cultural differences to gain a style of thinking similar to that of local nationals and become comfortable with the local culture. They receive a stipend of roughly $60,000, as well as their regular salary, to do as they please. In return, they are asked to keep records and form impressions of the area and contribute that information to the Group's database.

Since 1990, almost 1,500 people have been sent to 50 countries. This allows the Group to evaluate how well their employees will do in that area before they actually start making business decisions. It also allows the employee to become more familiar with local language and customs in a less stressful learning environment. Employees also often meet local staff members during the course of their stays. This allows them to establish relationships outside of the office first, thus allowing both parties to start working together more easily if they are reassigned to that area in the future.

As with *nemawashi*, the process of preparing a world-class workforce takes time and patience. Often the process of cross-cultural skill building takes more time than companies are willing to give their people. By using this unique approach, Samsung is allowing its employees to prepare for their future assignments in new markets at a comfortable pace.

Another important area of training that Samsung is engaged in is its MBA program. The program has two aims: to provide higher level education for employees in-country or to help employees complete higher-level education overseas. This newly adopted system is open to manager and deputy general manager applicants.

The company provides full support, dispatching the participant and family overseas to receive MBA degrees in either social or technical areas. Participants and their families receive predeparture training before leaving and are supported by the company when they arrive in the United States. The goal of the Overseas MBA program is to help employees develop their international business sense and crisis management skills.

In-country, Samsung offers the Techno-MBA. The program, which was designed in cooperation with the Korea Advanced Institute of Science and Technology (KAIST), is aimed at developing supervisors in manufacturing who have thorough knowledge of business, technology, and information systems. In the first year, students work with the sponsoring organization as consultants on significant management problems and prepare detailed oral and written recommendations. After completing the core and advanced major courses, participants take part in business projects that combine theory and practical knowledge with business skills to solve top-level management problems. The major areas of emphasis include new product management, strategic management, and international business negotiation. The final stage of this program concludes with the student writing and defending a dissertation.

The Regional Specialist Program and the MBA Program are good examples of Samsung's commitment to education and the creation of a world-class workforce. There are also several other programs that are currently going on that deserve mention.

Globalization Training

This training includes overseas work skills and language use skills. It is divided into *globalization training* and *foreign language training*. The *globalization training* consists of six courses, including courses for those in overseas business divisions (in Korea), those who are to be sent on overseas assignments, and those who have returned from overseas assignments.

Management Development Courses

Management Development can be broken down into Basic Training and Developmental Training. Basic Training starts with new recruits and is also given to newly promoted managers, general managers, and directors. In addition, special seminars are part of this category. Developmental Training focuses on the 21st Century Leadership Course and the 21st Century CEO Course.

21st Century Leadership Course

This course for general managers focuses on management skills, leadership skills, self-management skills, and problem-solving skills and is required before promotion to a senior management position. The course lasts six months, six weeks of which is conducted at an overseas location.

21st Century CEO Course

This course is for senior managers (director and above) who will lead Samsung into the 21st century. Trainees learn about history, future society, applying Samsung's *New Management* policy, languages, and computers.

Work Skill Courses

These programs teach specific work-related skills to help employees perform their jobs better. For marketing people, there is the Marketing Specialist Course with special seminars. Production and quality control people attend the Production Specialist Course or Quality Control Specialist Course, while procurement personnel take the Procurement Specialist Course. People working in Personnel or Training Departments take part in the Personnel Specialist Course or Training Specialist Course. Another program, the Specialist Secretary Course, is aimed at secretaries.

FUTURE TRENDS

Samsung is a good example of how some Korean companies are preparing for the future and their related training needs. However, Korean companies will be faced with many new hurdles during the next five years. Globalization will have an even greater effect on training. Currently, too much time is being spent on superficial areas. Many believe that learning the customs and manners of other cultures is enough to get by on. Of course, language is also seen as important, and commitment to that area is growing, but subjects such as diversity, team building, and executive management skills are often ignored. Most companies do not see these issues as very important. They generate just enough mal-o-man (lip-service) to appear politically correct, but, in fact, there is little known about how these issues are going to change the way they do business.

For training programs to succeed, many Korean companies still have to address the issue of globalization and what it really means regarding their future. They will have to develop the necessary infrastructure to facilitate programs as well as to train employees in how to optimize their performance. To date, Korean companies have done well at producing hardware (i.e., facilities), but there is a definite lack of software (i.e., effective programs). For programs to be effective, they must be tailored to reflect the company's corporate culture as well as their strategic needs. Furthermore, language training must continue, but more responsibility must be shouldered by individuals. Although language proficiency has increased greatly during the past five years, a concerted effort must be made at all levels of the educational system before any real gains are realized.

CHAPTER 13

Southeast Asia

Asma Abdullah
Specialist In Intercultural Training,
Management And Education, Malaysia

CURRENT ISSUES

The influences that are affecting the development of human resources in most organizations in Southeast Asia are many and varied. As many Asian economies, particularly Malaysia, embrace industrialization and seek to cultivate and nurture a productive and competitive work culture, they also have to face the challenges of business globalization and rapid advances in information technology. In simultaneously industrializing and globalizing, the focus on developing the quality of the nation's human resources has now become a top priority on the agenda.

With speed and value-added services becoming sources for a competitive edge in this borderless world, Asian economies have to explore new and creative ways to develop new business initiatives that are globally responsive. Equally significant as the boundaries of the world begin to shrink through electronic media and travel, the culture element has now become an important ingredient for organizations that want to have a competitive edge. To enhance global consciousness and communication, cultural literacy is now considered a valued currency—a global prerequisite as managers all over the world have to deal with various levels of workplace diversity—from physical, social, professional, and functional levels to variations in cultural values and their influence on business behaviors in order to remain connected.

For the field of human resource development, these forces of change would require the local workforce to be exposed to different workstyles and to internalize new work-related values and skills to enable them to respond to the competitive demands of the global workplace. The key challenge for any human resource development efforts, therefore, lies in the ability of management to develop local technical and managerial expertise to a level that allows them to be more responsive and creative in fulfilling the needs of both domestic and international business settings.

As countries and economies in this region begin to grow and expand internally and across borders, both foreign-based and locally led organizations have to review and update their own training and development programs. Managers must look five or more years ahead to the shape of their organization to ensure that they are developing local managerial talent who are well-equipped with the essential skills to motivate and lead their workforce to meet that growth.

Management Development

In most organizations, whether in the public or private sector—the outcome of any human resource development effort is to enable the individual employee to become a more effective and valued contributor on the job. In the Asian work setting, particularly, this effort and investment has to ensure that the well-trained employee remains a loyal contributor who is willing to serve the organization for a long period of time.

Over the last few years, the development of management skills has been perceived mainly as the transfer of techniques based on concepts, theories, and learning materials from Western business schools, and secular and linear management systems and practices. While quantitative techniques and methods of production, finance, and accounting are easily transferable, those related to the softer and affective aspects of human development of leadership, decision making, negotiating, motivation, and communication may not go so well across cultures. Techniques about qualitative management practices are often harder to transfer than quantitative ones as they rest heavily on the values and underlying assumptions of a particular culture. Hence, management is simply not one of techniques and rational methods—it is about accomplishing work objectives in the social and cultural contexts of an existing Asian society.

Seen through western logic, Asian values and management practices relating to the human dimension may not make sense unless one also has cultural sense.

The field of human resource development (HRD), which includes training, has been gaining attention as Malaysian-based organizations seek the expertise of both local and foreign-based consultants. Either through personalized and tailor-made or commercially developed programs, these *experts* bring along with them various courses related to

- Managerial Styles and Practices
- Performance Appraisal Systems and Counseling
- Communication and Assertiveness Training
- Sensitivity Training
- Managing Interactions
- Team Building
- Leading
- Motivation

Most of these training programs are very much the products of thinking of a highly urban, individualistic, less hierarchical and often competitive work setting, which often permeates corporations in America more than the Asian workplace.

When these products of western thinking are converted into skills and techniques and made available in the training rooms in Asia, they are often used without much interpretation and adaptation for the local setting. Hence the importation of foreign management techniques will make Malaysians less inclined to explore and test their own local-based theories, which are congruent and in harmony with local values.

The challenge for HRD professionals in Malaysia is, therefore, to question the applications of imported techniques back at the workplace and to initiate research and development on strategies and materials about managing and developing people in the local context. To embark on this undertaking, they have to overcome the "tyranny of their past learning" about management practices that are based on a set of values and underlying assumptions derived from a more western, individualistic, and less hierarchical work setting.

Merely adopting foreign-based management and training techniques without any adaptation will only reduce the role of HRD professionals to becoming mere peddlers of thinking and training based on a different cultural context. The task ahead for human resource professionals is to revisit their own cultural symbols and values instead of taking them as predefined or given and use them to evaluate any imported materials so they reflect both global and local perspectives (see Figures 13.1 and 13.2).

Figure 13.1
Values Underlying Training Materials

Values Underlying Training Materials	
Western-Based	**Malaysian-Based**
Individualism	Collectivism
Assertiveness	Loyalty and trust
Forcefulness	Cooperation
Openness	Politeness
Directness face-to-face	Indirectness
Self-actualization	Face saving
Task orientation	Relationship orientation
Logic	Respect for hierarchy
Specificity	Tolerance

Figure 13.2
Values Underlying Management Practices

Concepts	More Malaysian	More Western
Coaching	Facework, feelings	Information, data
Counseling	Nurturing parent and child	Adult to adult
	Relationship based	Task orientation
	Flexibility, indirect in action plans	Time-specific, direct immediate action
	Multiple roles	Professional role
	Shame and group harmony	Guilt and self-esteem
	Person to person	Face to face
	Third-party intervention	One on one
Communication	High context	Low context
	"What is said may not be what is meant to be"	"What you see is what you get"
	Indirect and subtle	Direct and to the point
	Wholistic	Compartmentalized, linear
	Softness (tone, vocal)	Clarity, openness
	Local polite system	Assertiveness, frankness
	Less disclosure	Self disclosure
Conflict	Avoidance, compromise	Competing
	Suppressed anger	"Let's get it out"
	Feelings, sensitivities	Logic and verbosity
	Collaboration	Confrontation
	Relationship: long-term	Task, result: short-term
Controlling	Authority centered	Self-control
	General	Specific
	Shame, external driven	Guilt, internal driven
Leadership	Power in the person	Power in the office
	Informal power and influence	Position power
	Total character	Skills competencies
	Humility, hand in hand	Assertiveness
	Respect elders deference	Ahead of others
	Relationship, trust	Result oriented
	Seniority, maturity	Achievement oriented
	Consensus seeking	Combative
	Admiration, role model	Self-actualization
	Social, national responsibility	Individual " Me" orientation
	Patriarchical/paternalistic	
Motivating	Affiliation	Self-actualization
	Relationship based	Task orientation
	Group fulfillment	Individual achievement

	Spiritual meaning	Worldly based
	Success in terms of rapport with family, friends, associates	Success in terms of material symbols
Organizing	Benevolent	Democratic
	Autocratic	Participative
	Organic	Mechanistic
	Circuitous, wholistic	Linear, Sequential, Step by step
Planning	Polychromic	Monochromic
	Flexible	Timeliness, deadlines
	Circular, global	Linear, pragmatic
Staffing	Nepotism, support network	Competency based
	Favoritism	Fairness
	Group loyalty	Equal opportunity
	Long-term commitment	Objectivity
	Social obligation	Individual based
Team building	Consensus seeking	Winning the game
	Subjugation of self	Problem solving
	Family oriented	Role clarification
	Gotong royong, mesyuwarah	Task orientation
	Spontaneity	Boundary definition
	Voluntariness	Specificity
	Relationship orientation	Task orientation
	Spiritual fulfillment	Individual achievement
	Collectivism	Individual future based
	Rapport with group	Goal driven

Current Training Practices

For most organizations, the current focus is to provide opportunities for training and developing the workforce to acquire the relevant knowledge and skills to become effective contributors.

In a recent study on *Human Resources and Priorities for Increasing the Competitive Edge* conducted by the Malaysian Institute of Personnel Management, it was concluded that for the long term:

> The organizations that gain a competitive advantage from human resource initiatives will be those which successfully forge business partnerships between HR and line management to integrate HR capabilities with business needs.

Among the top seven HR priorities the study highlighted are the following:
- Workforce productivity and quality of output.
- Teamwork.
- Employee education and training.
- Workforce planning—flexibility and deployment.
- Information systems.
- Performance appraisal.
- Employee participation and empowerment.

Overall, the survey suggests that successful HR management in the year 2000 will focus on four major elements, which are as follows:
- Responsiveness to a more competitive marketplace and to changing business structures including the greater use of sophisticated technology.
- Close links to the organization's strategic plans.
- Focus on productivity, quality, customer satisfaction, teamwork, and workforce flexibility and development.
- The shared responsibility of line managers and HR specialists.

Similarly, in an earlier and separate effort in 1992, the Malaysian Institute of Management also conducted a survey on Malaysian managers and values. Listed here are the top 10 managerial values among 2,000 respondents:
1. Goal clarity
2. Cooperation
3. Decisiveness
4. Commitment
5. Achievement
6. Accountability
7. Shared wisdom
8. Performance merit
9. Continuous improvement
10. Meeting deadlines

In analyzing the available list of vendor-offered courses in the market, most of them tend to focus on skills building from communications to report writing and from negotiations to personal peak performance.

But it is more important for the years ahead for management to provide opportunities for their workforce to benefit from learning and education through company-sponsored activities. Through these efforts the workforce would be in a continuous learning posture to take advantage of new management thinking and technology.

With the current drive for quality, customer-focused, and value-added service, all knowledge workers have to continuously improve their work processes in an effort to more quickly respond to their customers with better service and personalized attention.

As local-based companies expand and move from simple import-export relationships to those demanding an integrated approach to business, the focus of management development programs in Malaysia is on acquiring knowledge, skills, and techniques that are able to withstand the forces of change and their various accompanying values. In this effort, HRD professionals must be culturally literate to innovate new and contextually appropriate training interventions and combine the values often associated with a work-oriented culture and a people and cultural orientation. Strategic responses and initiatives for enabling the workforce to acquire a repertoire of skills to comfortably communicate and do business across borders must be high on the training agenda of both the human resource development professionals and their clients.

In planning and developing these initiatives, it would be useful for both local and foreign HRD professionals working in Malaysian organizations to consider the following steps in responding to the seven HR initiatives stated earlier and the development of management skills related to the 10 managerial values:

1. Needs analysis
   There has to be a thorough needs analysis of the level of knowledge and required competencies in a particular organization. This means that they have to be adept at conducting surveys and gathering information of the knowledge and skills deficiencies of the workforce. Both quantitative and qualitative approaches should be used to obtain the relevant information about skills gaps within the organization. For example, conducting a training needs analysis should not only include a pen and pencil survey and face-to-face form of interaction; it should also look at the underlying values and assumptions of the organization and to what extent there is a fit between the individuals and the organization they belong to. When courses are designed, new skills, which are in harmony with the values of the workforce, have to be explored, tested in the classroom, and applied back on the job.

2. Organizational climate

   In implementing a specific training program in the organization, there is a need to go beyond accommodating the felt needs as identified by their clients. In attempting to suggest solutions through training programs, it is pertinent to look at the organizational structure and climate, as these can deter employees from demonstrating the newly acquired skills learned in the training rooms. For example, a hierarchical-based organization may not be able to provide a motivation for employees to feel empowered and be openly critical of the organization.

3. Influence of culture

   As discussed earlier, the influence of local culture when introducing training interventions in an organization can no longer be ignored. The hidden dimension of culture or roots—values and underlying assumptions of the people in a particular society—has to be studied and recognized.

   Without understanding these elements, the new knowledge and skills observed among learners in the sanctity of the classroom will only anchor themselves into old and traditional practices, orientations, and beliefs. No change in the expected behavioral outcomes are observed— only forms of change providing an illusion that there is a change, but the underlying processes continue to remain the same. Hence, HRD professionals have to recognize the impact of cultural values on business behavior and how these values are manifested at the workplace through managerial practices of leading, communicating, motivating, planning, organizing, resolving conflict, and negotiating.

4. Training interventions

   HRD professionals need to examine the corporate culture of their clients' organizations. The underlying values and assumptions of the organization they work in and how employees are adjusting to them are key elements to consider when developing any training interventions that are congruent with the culture of the organization and the values of the workforce. They have to recognize that organizations bring along with them the cultural baggage of senior managers and shareholders in the form of systems, procedures, techniques, and ways of developing human resources. For example, in conducting a Performance Appraisal and Counseling program, HRD professionals have to examine the values of their clients and their degree of comfort in providing face-to-face feedback based on an individual performance system.

5. Work Orientation

   There has to be a concerted effort on the part of organizations to develop among the workforce a synergistic work orientation which incorporates the best of both Western and Eastern perspectives of doing business. This means that the workforce will, in addition to their basic education degree, continue to learn throughout their working lives. Additional resources to enable the workforce to acquire the following knowledge and skills should be made available by the organization:

   • Specific industry skills that cover technical and professional areas.
   • Development geared toward an industry or profession.
   • Supporting skills in management, negotiation, entrepreneurship, communication, and public relations to equip them for such work.
   • Mastery in more than one language—especially competence in the English language for business writing and presentations.
   • Business and work ethics to develop a sound work and business culture.
   • Opportunities for demonstrating leadership proclivities for global and local work settings.

6. Cultural Surgery

   Equally important, HRD professionals in Malaysia will also have to critically assess some of the values of Asian society as they may become impediments to their efforts to be globally connected. This means they have to perform *surgery* by recognizing which existing cultural values and work processes tend to reduce organizational efficiency and effectiveness in getting things done. They have to question the usefulness of those beliefs and outmoded practices that are incongruent with new aspirations and invalid in the present times. It is only when these practices are discarded that there can be room for new values and practices to take shape. Hence any extreme interpretation of Asian values—such as blind loyalty, autocratic decision-making, excessive protocol and ceremonies, unquestioning obedience, indirect approach in communication, conflict avoidance, and current work and managerial practices that manifest of some form of "residual feudalism" and can militate against the sharing of information, knowledge, and experience—may have to be downplayed.

7. Research and Development

   HRD professionals have to engage in continuing research on the value drives of people in organizations. They have to design, develop, and implement training programs that are based on a global orientation for local delivery and begin to incorporate theories, insights, and perspectives of leading and motivating the workforce based on values of respect for elders and those in positions of authority, a more collectivist orientation to getting things done, and a more hierarchical and larger power distance relationship between superiors and subordinates. Also important is to develop constructive and nonconfrontational mechanisms, particularly in Asian organizations, for top management to receive regular feedback. The use of 360° feedback is one form of localizing a management practice that provides upward feedback that is not face-to-face. It is also nonthreatening since a third party is used to convey valuable information that is seen to be more objective and fair.

A Supervisory Development Project

Introduction

The involvement of line management in the training process within an organization has been well documented in management literature both locally and abroad. For in-house HRD professionals, having line managers design and participate as up-front presenters is perhaps a luxury that few companies can afford. But when support and commitment from line management is demonstrated, it can enhance training and make it more relevant and congruent with the business needs of the organization. In addition, training will be more focused on the needs of the customer and help communicate to the organization the importance of integrating line and staff functions in delivering a service.

This Southeast Asian case study is an illustration of an organizationwide training effort for developing and training first-line supervisors in an overseas affiliate of a U.S. multinational organization. It brought together a multidisciplinary team of managers, supervisors, and professionals from different job functions to effectively collaborate with the training section to design and implement a tailor-made training program for a specific target audience. The project involves a number of critical steps: a training needs assessment, design of learning and training activities, development of content materials, and implementation, and evaluation of the intended outcomes.

Although the evaluation step has not been fully completed—the approach used by the organization to implement the project can serve as a guide for future trainers or consultants to re-examine their role when introducing an organizationwide training intervention. The perspective of an internal HRD specialist who was involved in the project from inception to implementation forms the focus of this study.

Background

The in-house first-line supervisory project was initiated by top management in the organization in 1990 in response to the growing need for both National and Expatriate managers to refine their supervisory knowledge, skills, and practices.

A Steering and Working Committee, consisting of 10 very experienced line and staff managers, was appointed to provide their wealth of experience and expertise to implement the project. The committee was led by the department manager of the largest department while the training personnel served as a secretary and HRD contact to members of the committee.

With this wealth of in-house expertise and experience, the multifunctional team reviewed, identified, and implemented a five-phase supervisory training matrix. Four of the five phases have been successfully completed. The last phase has just been piloted. At each phase of the project, the commitment and involvement of senior management was highly visible and commendably noted by the supervisory personnel.

It has to be reiterated that the key to any training effort in any large organization depends on a three-pronged approach, which is described as follows:
- The participant-supervisor, who is the target audience, must accept the fact that training is one of the solutions used to resolve a skills gap.
- The immediate-supervisor, who is the sponsor and client, must support the importance of training and provide constant feedback to the training process.
- The training section must be involved in coordinating training activities, locating the relevant materials and sourcing the right expertise for professional input.

The three parties must be involved in the process of implementing training so that it does not remain an isolated classroom event of the HRD group in the organization (see Figure 13.3).

The Training Cycle

In developing and implementing the supervisory project, the Steering Committee monitored various activities under five steps (see Figure 13.4).

Step 1: Training needs identification
Step 2: Program design
Step 3: Development of materials
Step 4: Implementation
Step 5: Evaluation

Various activities from Step 1 to Step 4 were implemented by members of the Committee. Because of their positions in the organizational hierarchy, members were also able to delegate some of the assigned work to their subordinates, thus enlarging the pool of in-house resources to work on the supervisory project.

Figure 13.3
Three Factors of Training Success

Figure 13.4
The Five Steps in the Training Cycle

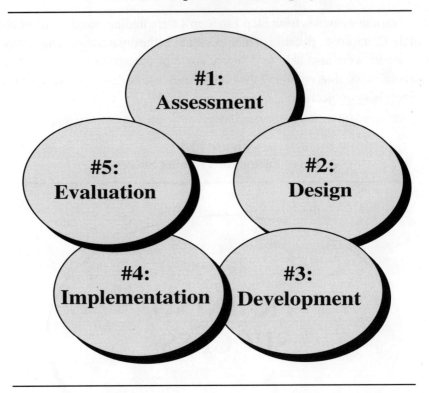

Step 1: Assessment

At the initial stage of the five-year project, the committee met to identify various activities and allocate responsibilities to implement the project. A budget was prepared and presented to management for approval. Additional resources in terms of contract personnel were also identified to support the work of the committee members in the following activities:

- An identification and description of first-line supervisors was made and included their job titles, salary groupings, total company experience, years of supervisory experience, number of people they supervised, and types of courses they have attended.

- Compilation of critical skills and qualities of a supervisor based on the feedback responses submitted by senior managers in the organization on seven key supervisory dimensions was assembled.
- A 56-item survey questionnaire based on the seven dimensions was designed and distributed to all supervisors, their immediate superiors, and subordinates. The questions were based on the seven skills dimensions critical to effective supervisory practices.
- Oral interviews with key managers and group discussions with homogenous (same level) groups consisting of supervisors, their immediate superiors, and subordinates were also held at various office locations.
- Data was gathered from written questionnaires and face-to-face and group-conducted interviews were analyzed. Recommendations based on the findings were presented to management for concurrence and subsequent follow-up actions.

Step 2: Program Design

During the design step, the committee members reviewed the planned activities to be conducted in implementing the project for supervisors. Two other activities that were carried out in this step were

- A Supervisory Development Process flowchart was created to systematically develop, train, and monitor the progress of supervisors to acquire the desired skills and qualities for effective job performance. As shown in Figure 13.5, the flowchart shows the supervisory development process and the need for collaboration between the supervisor, his immediate supervisor, and the training section in ensuring that the three-pronged approach is fulfilled.
- A five-phase supervisory training matrix was formulated to illustrate the segments of training and development for first-line supervisors. Phases 2 and 3 are courses where supervisors will have to complete 21 modules on various supervisory dimensions.

Step 3: Development

In developing the materials for all five phases, the Steering and Working Committee members were given the task of identifying training materials on the seven supervisory dimensions and including company-related training materials and activities to enhance the course curricula. The training personnel were designated to make available print materials, readings, videotapes, and manuals for members of the committee to review for relevance to supervisory knowledge and appropriateness to the culture of the organization. Commercially produced videotapes were purchased to enhance the learning of management concepts and techniques stressed in various modules.

Figure 13.5
Supervisory Development Process

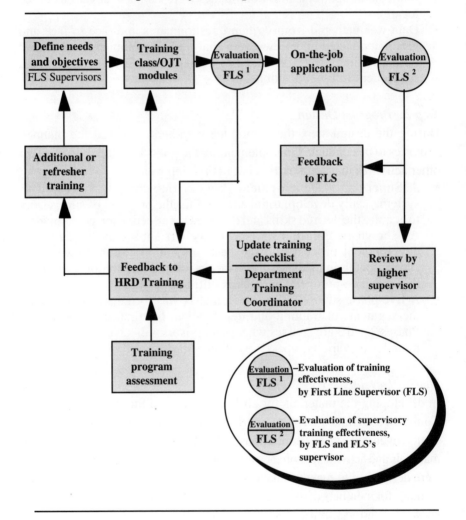

A line-up of senior managers was identified and approved by top management to serve as instructors cum facilitators to deliver the various prepared modules in Phases 2 and 3. An orientation session and face-to-face coaching sessions were organized to enable managers to receive useful pointers to assist them in facilitating the discussion when they deliver their respective modules in class.

As first-line supervisors are the first point of contact between employee and management, the Committee also prepared and compiled a set of manuals containing the relevant documents on policies and procedures to enable supervisors to be prepared in responding to questions on human resource issues.

Step 4: Implementation
The project activities covering the five phases were communicated to all levels of management through a series of briefing sessions. The two classroom courses were piloted and refinements made for subsequent instructors to facilitate the modules on their own. Instructional guidelines were also developed to assist line managers in conducting each module on their own. Five pilot sessions on Phases 2 and 3 were held before the courses were finalized to cover about 500 supervisory personnel from various departments in the organization.

In addition, the Committee used the professional services of an external consultant to conduct two of the modules to enrich and augment the use of in-house resources.

Step 5: Evaluation
The final step in the process of evaluation so far has only focused on reactions of participants as a result of classroom training. While both courses have received excellent ratings, line managers are currently upgrading the materials to keep them current and topical.

Lessons Learned

The collaborative approach in delivering training has made line managers become more familiar with the five-step cycle in implementing training as well as the learning materials used to develop supervisors in the organization. Their participation as upfront presenters in the classroom has increased their visibility and also provided first-line supervisors with first-hand knowledge and insights on how senior managers interpret organizational policies and practices in their day-to-day work.

The participation of senior managers in conducting training courses has now become a norm in the organization and is considered a key element in the transfer of management technology. It has permeated into other types of learning and training efforts as any up-date of materials used are also reviewed by line managers for consistency and relevance with current organizational realities.

Besides management presentations, line managers have also refined their facilitation skills and have received exposure to interactive learning approaches to make the class more participative and active in learning and training.

In summary, the project has benefited the organization in the following ways:

1. Initiated a more collaborative and partnership approach in delivering training to employees in the organization. Training is now firmly embedded in the organization, securing links to strategic objectives and permitting it to operate in a corporate context.

2. Enabled the training section to coordinate and conduct training courses by engaging the expertise of a pool of senior line managers who can facilitate discussions on a wide range of subjects related to managing people and work processes. They are able to share their own perspectives as they interpret their own understanding about management concepts and practices.

3. Generated a resource panel of management expertise who are able to articulate the mission, vision, and values of the organization and how they are implemented into day-to-day managerial practices and behaviors in the organization. They are able to model their talk by sharing some of their own best practices in managing the people dimension.

4. Exposed managers who have been selected to facilitate various modules to the range of learning materials and activities provided by the training section on making people and organizations learn. As they prepare to deliver the modules, they, too, will have to be kept up-to-date with new and current management literature on a wide range of topics.

5. Provided an opportunity for line managers who facilitated the modules to interact closely and exchange views with supervisors on current organizational issues in the sanctity of a learning community. They are able to articulate directly their observations and frustrations by senior managers.

6. Expanded the realm of expertise and influence of the training personnel and added the internal consultancy role in their day-to-day work. They are more familiar with issues and concerns faced by managers and are better positioned to provide appropriate responses when their services are being sought. They are also in a more advantageous position to convey any feedback on organizational issues articulated in supervisory courses to nonsupervisory personnel.

The Supervisory Development project has been looked upon as a commendable effort between line management and staff personnel in delivering a key service to its internal customers. It has gained a significant milestone in integrating managers into the training function. The project has clearly communicated the importance of tapping internal expertise to benefit the organization and drive home the point that training is and will always remain a line responsibility.

FUTURE TRENDS

With the increasing focus on speed, flexibility, and quality becoming the standards of the global workplace, the Southeast Asian workforce must become more responsive to various sources of change. HRD professionals must review the Western-based techniques that they have been using and initiate practices that are rooted in their own traditions and values to promote productive and creative endeavors. Alternatively, they should synergize managerial practices that are a blend of both Western and Eastern values so as to remain globally connected and locally responsive.

Management practices and training strategies can only be meaningful to the workforce when they are fully anchored in local roots to promote and increase workplace effectiveness.

Two distinctive trends are emerging in Southeast Asian companies as people are trained for new markets open for business. The two trends are interconnected around customer service issues. Asian businesses will need to (1) train their people in customer service and (2) train employees to understand the cultures of their customers—first the cultures of Europe and Latin America and then the cultures of the Middle East and Africa—as sales and distribution of products and services expand. Pacific Rim companies have been looking to American consultants who have much experience in these areas to assist them with these important issues.

CHAPTER 14

Japan

Tadashi Iwaki, Director
Kevin Reynolds, Training Consultant
Globalinx Corp.

CURRENT ISSUES

In the 90s the worldwide economic growth slowed down and the direct investment of industrialized countries dramatically decreased. However, foreign capital investment to Asia steadily grew. According to the Bank of International Settlements (BIS), direct investments to Asia in the early 80s was $4.9 billion, $13.7 billion in the late 80s, $20.2 billion in 90, $32.7 billion in 92, and $47.5 billion in 93.

After the Plaza Agreement in September 1985, the value of the yen appreciated and Japanese companies accelerated their investments into the Association of Southeast Asian Nations (ASEAN). Accordingly, the investments promoted ASEAN's rapid industrialization, especially in exporting industries (see Figure 14.1).

Japanese companies operating in ASEAN have established their business networks for local procurement of parts and raw materials as well as distribution networks for selling products. They have also started networking their Japanese headquarters/factories and major overseas branches in East Asia to promote the international division of business operations. Japanese companies have selected the NIES as their regional manufacturing office. In addition to these roles, Hong Kong has become the front door to mainland China. The role of the Japanese is to support and provide machinery equipment and parts that were not available locally.

Japan has now become the marketplace for products and parts that the regional companies manufacture. Through this process, the development mechanism in East Asia has been established.

Figure 14.1
Japanese Direct Investments to Overseas

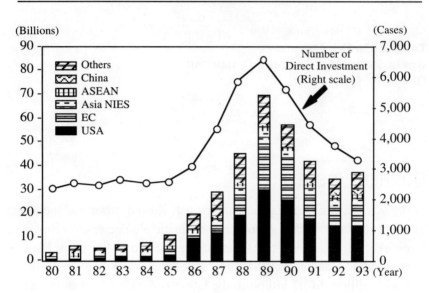

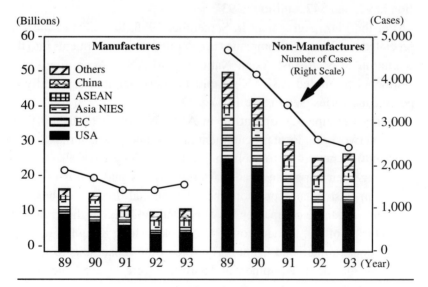

Source: Ministry of Finance

Due to the further appreciation of the yen in 1993, Japanese companies started to shift their manufacturing to China, Vietnam, and India, in addition to ASEAN. The investments to China accelerated from 1992 due to the innovation of Chinese business and the opening of the economic policy by the Chinese Government. In 92 the amount of investments from Japan into China was \$0.71 billion (a 33.3 percent increase over the previous year) and \$1.32 billion (an 86.5 percent increase) in 93. This tendency continued in 94. Another remarkable trend is the increase of direct investments by small and mid-sized Japanese enterprises, mostly by the manufacturing industries (see Figure 14.2).

Figure 14.2
Direct Investments of Japanese
Small to Mid-sized Enterprises

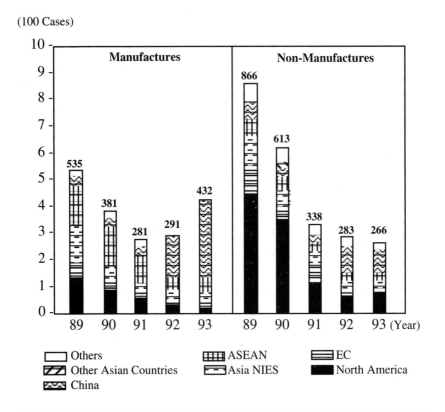

Source: Ministry of Mid & Small Size Enterprises

Those companies that started business in the late 80s in ASEAN are now getting into their stride. In other words, they are now at the stage when they can become more independent from their Japanese headquarters. As this trend develops, these companies are facing difficulties selecting the appropriate Japanese managers. One reason is the shortage of managers who have the capability to supervise experienced local national staff. Compared to their work in Japan, managers assigned to work overseas are required to work at two to three levels higher in terms of management skills. The HRD manager of NIPPONDENSO CO., LTD. (top producer of electronic and electrical parts for automobiles), says, "Sending third-generation managers to any overseas office is the most difficult task for both the company and the individual. This is because of the local national employees' growth. They expect a higher level of Japanese manager. If the manager does not do the right job, they may think, why do we need Japanese managers? This is the most critical issue of our company." This kind of statement is often heard from HRD people in other companies, also.

Another concern of HRD managers comes from the business/manufacturing shift to China, Vietnam, or India. Expatriates, as well as HRD managers, are concerned about the kind of training programs that are necessary for these regions. A middle-aged salesman of Omron Corp. (top manufacturer of control components) has received an unexpected assignment to Hong Kong. He has worked purely in the domestic market for over 25 years. He cannot speak Chinese or English. "How can I communicate with Chinese people? I have to go because my client had to go out of Japan due to the high value of the yen. My client needs to receive the same service in Hong Kong that they received in Japan, " he said. This case may be a little unusual; however, there are many people who have to go to these regions without sufficient preparation, not only in language but also in other areas.

Moreover, from the early seventies until the mid-eighties, English language training was just about the only internationalization training that Japanese business people had before going overseas. An additional list of cultural do's and don'ts, although useful, was hardly enough to prepare an internationally inexperienced worker for life in a foreign country. Emphasis was placed on technical training rather than actual communication skills. Consequently, many business people found themselves faced with difficulties when working in their second language.

An engineer with Mitsubishi Electric says: "When I was in Germany the local engineers were far stronger than I was. By that I mean I just ended up agreeing with whatever request they made to me, even if I knew I shouldn't have. I just didn't know how to negotiate with them." An engineer from Omron says: "Often I say something to a foreign colleague and his face changes. He is angry and I have no idea what I said to make him angry."

Nippon Telegraph and Telephone (NTT) uses assertiveness and presentation skills training to prepare employees for training assignments overseas. In previous years, NTT engineers found it difficult to participate in training courses run by overseas carriers. In particular, the Japanese found themselves in a silent minority when trainees from other countries asked many questions of their instructors. Often unable to understand (despite years of English language training), the Japanese participants felt isolated and frustrated. They wanted to interrupt and ask questions, but they didn't know how. To add to their difficulties, trainees from other countries could describe their own companies and the state of the telecommunications market in their countries. The Japanese trainees could not. Assertiveness skills training shows the trainees how to fully participate in meetings and discussions, while presentation skills training gives the students confidence to talk about their company and the Japanese telecommunications marketplace.

Mitsubishi Electric (MELCO) schedules regular presentation and negotiation skills training courses, which anyone can attend if their English level is good enough. MELCO also organizes predeparture training courses for overseas candidates. These predeparture training courses concentrate on assertiveness communication techniques but also incorporate negotiation and presentation training. The English level of the students varies from competence to almost no ability, and the targeted countries vary from Asia to America. This presents real problems for the trainers. The students are going overseas and so they need training in English, but they are not all going to the same place and some of them cannot understand a word the trainer is saying. The solution that MELCO uses is to have bilingual materials and to use a back-up Japanese trainer to translate as necessary. Note that MELCO does *not* want the whole course taught in Japanese, as they feel the students need to get used to having to work in a second language. MELCO also tries to arrange for many of the group to be going to the same country or area. For example, in a group of 15 students, seven may be going to Europe and the United States, and eight may be headed for Thailand or Singapore. The group comes together for the lectures but then splits into two sections for the role-plays, with an American role-playing in English for one group and a Thai role-playing in Japanese for the second group. In this way, everyone experiences what it is like interacting with foreigners and is better prepared for their overseas assignments. A student commented: "Last month I went to Chicago on a business trip. In meetings with native speakers I could hardly understand anything. I was panicking. But after this training course, I feel confident about going back there on my three-year assignment. Thank you." Music to the ears of a tired trainer.

Sanwa Bank schedules four predeparture training courses a year. The courses are a combination of assertiveness communication skills and human resource management. The students spend three days learning and practicing assertiveness communication techniques and then two days applying these skills in situations involving local staff for their assigned countries. Most of Sanwa's overseas assignees will be managers, so learning how to deal effectively with local staff is a priority for them. The students learn how to run a performance appraisal interview, how to reprimand staff, and how to fire staff when necessary. The human resource management section is designed to prepare the students for what will actually happen in their day-to-day lives as managers overseas.

Texas Instruments Japan

Texas Instruments faces a different challenge. As an American company in Japan, the local staff are Japanese, while those on overseas assignments are mainly from the United States and are typically at senior management level. Texas Instruments Japan (TI Japan) was founded in 1968. TI Japan's main line of business is the research and development (R & D), design, production, and sale of semiconductors. It has about 5,100 employees spread over 10 sales offices, five production factories, and five design and R&D centers throughout Japan.

TI Japan conducts meetings in English, the common language in the company. Even if all the members in a meeting are Japanese, presentations are still made in English. Local staff must make presentations in English on their department's performance and goals for the coming year. However, the quality of presentations varies from person to person. "The quality of a presentation not only reflects the quality of that person's work but also has an effect on an employee's promotion prospects," says Shinichi Onuki, Training and Organizational Effectiveness Development Manager with Texas Instruments Japan.

The gap between good and bad presentations is obvious even in meetings involving only Japanese staff, but the gap is more serious in the case of multinational situations. Very few Japanese people are born presenters. However few they are, those who can give a clear and persuasive presentation naturally to Americans or other nationals receive a good performance appraisal and are promoted faster than their colleagues. People once thought that this kind of skill was a given talent, and so could not be shared or taught effectively. Recently, however, TI Japan has come to realize that presentation skills is one of the areas where Japanese people must improve.

As a first step, TI Japan started using presentation skills training courses (in English) from Globalinx Corp. for managers and employees who need to present to non-Japanese people. As a second step, they need to expand this course in Japanese to everyone in TI Japan as one of their basic training programs.

Generally speaking, Japanese business people do not like to speak in meetings. The fundamental Japanese mentality means that people hesitate to assert themselves in front of their seniors. In the Japanese context, people who assert themselves are regarded as immature and are not respected by others. The Japanese unconsciously feel that they should not contradict senior personnel, and they try to show a kind of modest respect. TI Japan employees are no different, and they often act accordingly in front of American management in meetings.

However, assertiveness is an important attitude and skill that Japanese people need to improve on. TI Japan staff are required to use assertive communication skills in everyday business situations. Assertiveness training is, therefore, required. An Assertive Communication Development Course was begun in January 1995 for workers whose English level, especially speaking ability, is advanced. Therefore, at the moment, many TI Japan employees are excluded from the program because of the language difficulties. A program in Japanese is now being developed and will be implemented, so that many Japanese speaking people can participate in the program.

NEC Corp.

NEC Corp. (NEC) is one of the most globalized enterprises in Japan. NEC is famous for computers, communication equipment, and electronic equipment and devices. It now has about 41,000 employees in Japan and about 25,000 employees overseas. NEC has manufacturing, sales, and software service offices throughout the world (140 in Japan and 78 overseas).

In 1969, *internationalization* became a core management issue. Since then, NEC's overseas business activities have expanded. In 1980, its overseas sales represented 30 percent of total sales. In that year, the number of Japanese expatriates was approximately 1,000, and that number was expected to double a few years later. At that stage, international staff training became a critical issue for management.

In 1980, NEC established the *International Training Center* under which international management training, language training, and international business knowledge training were integrated to meet fast-paced international business developments. In 1983, the NEC Institute of Management, Ltd. was established in order to take care of the training needs for NEC and NEC's group companies. In 1987, the International Training Center was merged into this Institute.

International Training

NEC has the following three goals for international training:
1. Internalization of the Whole Organization.
2. Reinforcement of International Business.
3. Reinforcement of Overseas Strategic Position.

In order to cope with each level, NEC has prepared a wide range of training programs. Figures 14.3 and 14.4 show an overview of the NEC international training program.

Figure 14.3
NEC's International Training Program

Person	Program
In Japan — **All Employees**	**International Business Series** **Communication Course** **Area Study Series**
International Business Operators	**International Management Series**
Overseas Expatriate	**Management Course** **Family Course** **Re-entry Course**
Overseas — **Local National Employees**	**Overseas Managers Program**

Figure 14.4
Overview of Programs

- International Management Series

For Overseas Expatriates	◆ International Management Case Study Course
◆ Management Course	◆ USA EEO Course
◆ Family Course	◆ Overseas Managers Program
◆ Re-entry Course	◆ Chinese Business Management Course

- International Business Series

◆ Trade Business Course	◆ International Accounting Course
◆ International Finance Course	◆ International Marketing Course
◆ International Insurance Course	◆ International Construction Course
◆ International Law and Contract Course	◆ International Manufacturing Course

- Area Study Series

◆ North American Business Course	◆ Middle/South American Business Course
◆ European Business Course	◆ Oceania Business Course
◆ Asian Business Course	◆ Chinese Business Course
◆ Middle East Business Course	

- Communication Courses

◆ English Speaking Courses	◆ Negotiation Courses
◆ Technical English Speaking Courses	◆ Cross-cultural Course for Foreign National Employees
◆ Technical Writing Courses	
◆ Business Writing Courses	◆ Dale Carnegie Courses
◆ Language Courses (Chinese, Thai, Korean, Vietnamese, Indonesian)	◆ Presentation Courses
	◆ Self-study Guidance

Basically, these NEC programs are for those who are anticipating or actually doing international business.

The Communication Programs are basically for people who need communication skills for business. In addition to the language programs, which include both speaking and writing, there are practical communication skills programs, such as presentation and negotiation. About 2,000 employees take communication programs each year. Besides these so-called compulsory programs, NEC offers a wide range of voluntary programs. About 3,000 people a year take the voluntary programs. Also

NEC runs cross-cultural awareness and communication programs for foreign national staff working in Japan. The purpose of the program is to help foreign national staff communicate better with Japanese supervisors and colleagues. This program takes place once or twice a year with approximately 15 participants representing 10 different nationalities.

The International Management Series is for overseas expatriates and staff who take overseas business trips. Employees who deal with international business in Japan supporting overseas business also take this training. The training objective is to improve international management competence for success in the global business environment.

The International Business Series provides special skills and know-how necessary for international business for example, understanding international rules and improving the knowledge and sense of international business administration. This series provides a very wide range of programs, as illustrated in the Figure 14.4. In order to run the programs more effectively, NEC uses external professionals.

In the **Area Study Series,** NEC divides global business operations into seven regions — North America, Asia, Europe, Mid-South America, Middle East, China and Pacific Ocean. For these programs, internal and external speakers give lectures on each region's economic trends, social issues, and cultural situations of NEC's business development.

Overseas Managers Training has been conducted since 1977 to reinforce the management abilities of individuals in strategic overseas business positions. Overseas managers come to Japan for this program to study NEC's corporate philosophy and basic policy of business operation. The program is run three times a year and about 25 overseas managers participate each time.

In addition, new types of training for overseas managers have been implemented. One of them is the European Regional Managers Training, which was held at a business school in London. One of the HRD managers at NEC Institute of Management states, "A similar training was held a couple of times in Asia, too. Since the globalization of the organization is evolving, this trend is a natural phenomenon in order to meet the local training needs. Beyond this kind of regional training, training across borders and organizations will be necessary. We need to change the training style so that management can adjust to the globalization wave."

Omron

Omron is a top manufacturer of control components, electronic fund transfer systems, and computer equipment. Leslie Webb, manager of internationalization training at Omron, says:

> The prospect of selecting and developing personnel with skills to work overseas can be daunting. I remember being in one meeting to discuss abilities needed by personnel sent from Japan to work in overseas factories. The manager of one of these factories was in Japan at the time, and he joined the meeting. He emphasized that assignees should have excellent management and leadership abilities. Usually overseas they have to work at a level one or two ranks above their position in Japan. So a supervisor sent from Japan will often be a department manager overseas. He said persons sent from Japan should also have had job rotation in two or three fields, such as Quality Assurance, manufacturing processes, and product technology. Plus they would need English skills and good interpersonal skills. One of the domestic managers in the meeting reacted, 'Yeah, and I wish we had some guys like that in Japan, too.'

Other abilities a manager should have when working overseas include the following:
- Ability to formulate long-term company vision and strategy.
- Ability to set clear business plans and objectives.
- Ability to understand and organize resources effectively.
- Ability to manage according to the abilities of local staff.
- Ability to train and develop local managers.
- Ability to control work and projects in process.
- Ability to identify and solve problems.
- Ability to network, with domestic and overseas contacts.
- Special knowledge related to the country to which he or she is assigned (tax law, labor law, debt management, business practices, and local distributor channels).
- Special knowledge of domestic operations (domestic distribution and logistics for overseas shipping, information systems, and design in Japan for products for overseas markets).

Mr. Webb feels that there is generally a shortage of excellent potential managers and executives in a company, but this shortage does not mean that persons with high potential should be kept in Japan. Take the example of a young assignee who had gone with a small team to build and start a new overseas factory and had been in charge of all kinds of jobs, from working with local building contractors, to negotiating with the government on import/export procedures, to recruiting and handling personnel, administration, and finance. The young engineer said, "In two years here I've had ten years of job experience in Japan." Mr. Webb adds, "Given the shortage of potential managers and executives, Japanese companies should look at the challenges of the overseas assignment as an excellent opportunity for management development."

A second role assignees have to play is providing leadership to make overseas companies attractive, enjoyable places to work. A few years ago Mr. Webb trained two men to go overseas for one of their factories. They were fairly young, in their mid-thirties. Both were friendly and active and took initiative in their work. Because the two were friendly and active, they had changed the factory atmosphere. It had become more lively, and people enjoyed their work more. Omron feels that this ability to lead, in the sense of making overseas companies lively, enjoyable places to work, is an important role for assignees.

A third role for assignees is the development of local staff. In terms of cost and effectiveness, it is more efficient for the Japanese to use local staff instead of expatriates for most management positions in overseas companies. But there is often a shortage of qualified local staff, especially in developing countries. So one of an assignee's major roles should be the education and development of local staff under him. Ideally, when he leaves, one of these staff members should be able to take over his position.

Finally, a fourth role for assignees is internationalization of the parent Japanese company. One way they can internationalize the parent company is to introduce know-how they acquired in their jobs overseas. Twice a year Omron has a training program for returnees from overseas. In this program the returnees make suggestions about how to improve the company's overseas operations. And they also list useful business practices that they experienced abroad and would like to transfer back to Omron Japan. For example:

- The way of conducting meetings (agenda, conclusions, and action decided for each item on the agenda).
- The high position (compared to Japan) and professionalism of female employees.
- The clear division of responsibilities and delegation of authority.
- The high efficiency of white-collar employees (compared to Japan), through use of voice mail, e-mail, and personal computers.

Besides transferring this know-how from overseas, Mr. Webb adds that returnees can make domestic workers more conscious of overseas business. One commonly expressed goal of Japanese companies is to get all employees to have an *international mind*. Many workers in a Japanese company often think only about the company's domestic operations and pay no attention to its overseas business. Product development and design, for example, is often done to meet only the specifications of domestic customers. The needs and specifications of overseas customers are ignored. Returnees can help to make their fellow workers aware of overseas business by asking questions such as: "How will this look from overseas? Will the specs for this new product being developed also meet overseas requirements?"

Omron has a pool of about 500 workers that are registered as international trainees. From this pool some employees will be selected to go overseas and work. At present Omron has only about 130 overseas assignees, so most people who are international trainees will not have the chance to go abroad. Mr. Webb says, "But even if most trainees do not have the chance to work overseas, we think many of them, especially in production, will have an important role to play in supporting overseas operations."

Mr. Webb sees four qualities as essential to international trainees, whether they are potential candidates for overseas work or people who will one day handle support from Japan for overseas companies. These qualities are:

1. Professional competence

When someone from Japan goes abroad, local staff usually will make judgments about him such as, "If you tell him about your problem, he can do something for you" or "That guy doesn't know anything." They judge a person above all for his job competence and performance. So when registering employees as international trainees, Omron requires first of all that they have superior job skills and performance.

2. Good communication skills in English or another language

From surveys of assignees, Omron found that one of their most common sources of frustration abroad is inability to communicate—not being able to get across what they want to say. Mr. Webb says: "At work, communication is essential to management. If a Japanese worker overseas cannot communicate with his local staff, he cannot manage them."

3. Cross-cultural sensitivity

Omron believes that an international trainee should understand the typical values and behavior of the Japanese and look at them objectively. He should not be ethnocentric, and he should not have a feeling of superiority vis-á-vis people of another culture. He should be willing to suspend judgment on the apparently strange behavior of people in other cultures until he understands it better.

4. Awareness of world events and trends

Persons involved in international business must be aware of what is going on in world politics and economics. This awareness is necessary also for socializing with colleagues or people outside the company. Mr. Webb adds: "Japanese salarymen often talk about their work or golf. But in socializing abroad people will talk more about current news and events, and people are expected to have their own opinions on these topics."

Development Of Managers And Production Personnel

"In Omron about 40 to 50 percent of our assignees are persons with manager rank in Japan," Mr. Webb says. "These persons have important responsibilities, yet often there is a shortage of managers in Japan who are able to work overseas. The same is true for production personnel. So in international training, special attention must be paid to developing qualified personnel in these two groups. In addition to English skills, support staff in Japan should have special training in fax writing because of the frequency of fax communication with overseas. They should also receive training in how to do job instruction in English or give a product explanation in English." See Figure 14.5 for details of Omron's International Training System.

FUTURE TRENDS

Japanese management is changing. What was once known as *collective management* is now giving way to a more Western approach. This may surprise many observers, who have often thought that the tremendous Japanese economic advances were based on the unique Japanese management system, and that somehow this system was better than its

Figure 14.5
Omron Corporation International Training System

Self-Development Courses (open to all employees)		
Correspondence Courses	Fax, Business, Technical Writing	TOEIC Test
Courses for International Trainees		
Managers		
International Business Lectures	English Conversation	English Interview Test
Optional Courses		
Production Personnel		
Global Production Lectures	Production Semi-Intensive	English Interview Test
Optional Courses		
Trainees for Chinese Business (under development)		
Study in China	Chinese Conversation	China Seminar
Trainees with Jobs Related to Overseas Business		
Presentation Skills	Negotiation Skills	Office Communication
Interpersonal Management	Business Semi-Intensive	
Optional Courses		
Young Trainees (Long-term Development)		
International Mind Seminar	Self-Development Sheet	TOEIC Test
Optional Courses		
Overseas Assignees		
English Intensive	Basic Management	KT Method
Pre-departure Training	China Pre-Departure Training	Returnee Training
Local Staff		
Basic Management	Omron Management Seminar	

Western counterpart. Whether that is true or not, changes are taking place in the organization of Japanese companies, and these changes are having a profound effect on the type of training that will be required in the future.

Collective management in Japan has sought to form a kind of collaborative society encompassing such concepts as the life-time employment system, an age-based seniority system, and the company labor union—all of which worked in harmony together. University graduates entered into this society and pledged their loyalty to the company, which in turn guaranteed life-time employment. Both the company and the employees had a sense of security knowing that they would be together for the entire working lives of the employees. This type of management/ organization used to seek employees who *value human relationships*, or *people who can be trusted to complete a given task*, or *people who work with all their might* (literal translation).

So the purpose of training for this type of management/organization was to
- Bond an employee to the company.
- Reinforce an employee's skills to meet the company's expansion goals.

Many employees worked outside their university disciplines, as companies provided complete product and technical training, or re-training, to ensure staff were fully competent in the section they were sent to. Employees spend only three to four years in one place before moving to another section, which was often in a different area of operations. Constant training and re-training in the company's products and business methods allowed these employees to move internally without significantly disrupting their careers.

Changes in Management Philosophy and Style

Collective management is collapsing rapidly these days. Job mobility, once unheard of, is becoming more common, especially among the younger generation. Actually, changing jobs occurred *inside* companies, and usually the decision was made by a manager rather than the employee. Although this is still in the transitional phase, younger business people are more likely to consider changing companies than their predecessors, who rarely moved from one company to another.

Salary schemes are also changing. An employee's salary used to be based on his age and number of years service in the company with biannual bonuses accounting for 50 to 60 percent of the total. Recently, however, more and more companies are choosing to pay their employees based on their job performance, resulting in people in the same age bracket receiving different incomes. The relationship between an organization and its employees is becoming more flexible as deregulation happens in the workplace.

New Training Requirements

With these philosophical and structural changes, Japanese management is beginning to look for different types of people and training. The employees they now want are individuals who already possess technical knowledge and skills in their own profession. Management is also trying to focus training more on the development of the individual as a business person, rather than simply training that person as an employee of the company.

Examples of this new training trend include *Mind Space Seminars*, *Self-Actualization Systems*, and *Mind Life* (all literal translations). These seminars help people to look back on their past lives and to look ahead to the future as a form of career planning. These kinds of programs used to be for middle-aged employees and became popular around the collapse of the Japanese bubble economy (circa 1991). The reason for the growth in this type of training was that the combined salaries for business people in the 40+ age range was a heavy burden, and so companies were looking for ways to encourage staff to leave of their own accord through planning their own lives (firing them was usually out of the question although transferring nonperforming staff to subsidiary companies was an often used option).

Today this type of training is becoming more popular for employees of any generation—not because companies want staff to leave en masse—but to encourage staff to be more individualistic and to have their own outlook on life rather than the one provided for them by the company.

Management Training

Changes in management training have been remarkable. *Leadership Training* used to be the only theme for training managers in the past.

However, programs such as *Strategic Thinking* and *Management Decision Making* are becoming more popular in order to cope with diversification and changes in the business environment. Communication skills such as *Presentation Skills* and *Assertiveness Training* are also becoming more popular since coordination skills are crucial for managers to manage the changing organization.

Training for Leading Employees and Female Employees

Programs for leading employees (four to eight years of experience) now include *Practical OJT Application Training, Business Leadership Training, Your Role in Managing the Organization, Your Role in Strategic Management,* and *Problem Solving Methods.* This type of training was previously reserved for more senior managers; however, most organizations now feel that it is too late to start developing these areas at such an age. Finding candidates for future managerial positions and providing those candidates with managerial experience now begins earlier in their careers.

Development programs for female employees used to be known as the *Office Manners Program* and, quite obviously, did not go far in developing the potential of the participants. This, however, is changing, too. Courses such as *Business Lady Career Course, Advanced Course for Female Employees,* and *Female Marketer Seminar* (again, literal translations) are typical programs for female employees. These courses are offered because female employees themselves are looking for workplaces where they can fully perform. As this trend emerges, more and more organizations are changing their attitude toward *Office Ladies* and look at them as business people who can contribute to the company's growth.

Conclusion

In the midst of chaos and change comes opportunity—the opportunity to help form a new international business world where knowledge and experience are globally shared. This ideal world may not become a reality within the next few years, but definite movement can be seen in this direction.

One of the major observations of performance research from around the world is the similarities in current issues and future trends—no matter which region you are viewing. Perhaps this should not be surprising as our world grows more closely knit. Two major factors contribute to this shared knowledge:

- The instantaneous transfer of information through technology.
- The expansion of multinational companies into major areas of the globe.

In analyzing the current worldwide issues and future trends, new challenges emerge. Some of these challenges are reflected in changing terminology. The American Society for Training and Development conducted an informal survey of leaders, staff, and training executives on old and new HRD terms resulted in the list found in Figure C.1

Figure C.1
HRD Terms

Old HRD Terms	New HRD Terms
Trainee	Learner
Employee	Performer
Continual change	Transformation
Quality improvement	Process reengineering
The transfer model of learning	The social model of learning
Training events	Self-directed learning on the job
Big training departments	Outsourcing training
Monoculturalism	Diversity
Trainers as teachers	Trainers as enablers of learning
The invention of new training technology	The application of technology
Big companies	Small companies
Individual workers	Teams
Functions	Processes
Leadership	Stewardship
Control	Empowerment
Local	Global
Robert Mager	John Seely Brown
Supervisor	Coach
Loyalty to organization	Loyalty to profession
Program evaluation	Valued-added contribution
Responsibility	Accountability
Workshops	Computer-based training
Direct	Facilitate
Evolution	Resolution
Lifetime employment	Lifetime employability
Competition	Collaboration
Performance appraisal	Performance management
Classroom	Learning center
Selling	Serving
Vendors	Partners
Work environment	Community
Off-site meetings	Teleconferences
Profits	Social responsibility
Matrix	Network
Mail	E-mail
Compliances	Ethics and principles
Training as a cost	Training as an investment

* *National Report on Human Resources,* November/December 1995

These terms representing current and future trends are indicative of transformations in human resource development and its place within the global organization.

The Human Resources Function

In the past, the main role of corporate human resources was to make sure that the right people were hired, trained, and promoted along with the development of policies and procedures to ensure that they were able to perform in a consistent manner. Human resources' success was measured by how well they could attract and retain the *best* people to make the proven formulas for success work in their companies.

Today much less reliance is placed on proven formulas for success, and more emphasis is on developing tactics that will result in employees who possess multiple competencies, can deal with rapid change, and adapt to different kinds of customer expectations. These employees must be able to handle the dramatic changes in organizations brought about by competition, more customer demands, information technology, process improvements, and downward pressure on costs.

There is a growing trend to involve human resources in the executive decision-making process to make major contributions in aligning human potential to the strategic focus of the organization.

Several emerging role changes are evident:

- Trainers will spend less time in the classroom and more time partnering with internal customers and managing external providers. Trainers are becoming internal consultants and are developing and expanding skills for this new role. As internal consultants, they will have to add new learning tools to their competencies.
- Line managers have more responsibility for training. Training delivery will continue to shift from training professionals to line managers, team leaders, and technical workers. Managers are becoming mentors and coaches for employees providing more on-the-job learning experiences.
- More training will be delivered through technology, just-in-time, or directly on-the-job.
- Executives are developing their global skills by participation in international seminars and visiting *foreign* companies as a part of the executive development process.
- Multinationals will also continue to increase the training for employees and joint venture partners wherever they are located.

- Many companies will hire a Chief Knowledge Officer (CKO) who is responsible for the dissemination of information and learning.

Success in this process will depend on
1. Alternative forms to deal with corporate bureaucracy.
2. Alternative ways of learning, understanding the new ways, and presenting them effectively to internal partners.
3. Educating the partners. (If the managers are responsible for their human resources, they need to know more about dealing with that issue).
4. HRD and managers together must contribute through their joint effort with performance improvement.

Work is changing, and as a result, training approaches need to shift in the same direction. What is already seen as a significant trend is that training is redefined from a one-time event, targeted to internal workers, to a process of lifelong learning including a company's customer/supply chain as well as their internal employees.

With the permanent redesign of organizations, individuals must learn to manage their own careers and develop the competencies needed for each opportunity. Human resource professionals are becoming more like agents managing a pool of talent programs, giving to career development a broad view and a new set of skills to be learned.

In a knowledge economy, knowledge capital must increase, and, as a result, companies will request on-demand, just-in-time learning experiences. Development of interactive instruction using computers and multimedia devices will grow steadily.

Managers will be more involved in learning and will have to become more familiar with the learning process and how to create a positive learning environment. As Peter Block says: "Learning will be the only job left to managers." Businesses will need new approaches to training and development because complex tactical and strategic tasks now require the assimilation of large amounts of new knowledge along with heavy workloads. These approaches will have to provide sequentially arranged, systematic, applied workplace training for individuals and small groups.

Clear linkage to corporate strategy is a must, and continuity and modularity are other important characteristics. A systems approach and integration with other human resource efforts are also more prevalent. For larger companies, the HRD function is being regionalized—where it is closer to the employee. A complex world with cultural and language differences does not allow for a centralized approach to HRD.

Changes are apparent in management thinking—from dealing with *manpower* to developing human resources. The human element becomes an essential, expensive, and mobile factor with constantly growing demands upon it: individuals are required to demonstrate a deeper level of competency in what they do, they must show greater willingness to increase their involvement in problem solving, and to display more responsibility towards all that occurs around them.

Both organizational development and training play a central role in this regard. Indeed, most organizations invest vast resources in presenting ideas and concepts, in the development of skills, and in providing the necessary tools. The joint challenge for both managers and instructors alike, is thus in building a training environment which creates an organic link between what is learned in the classroom and what happens on a practical daily basis.

Lifelong Learning

A growing market has brought to many area companies a new approach to training issues. Companies have often been seduced by *quick fix* programs and insisted on short-time vision and efforts. For example, companies suddenly decide they need to empower their employees or implement an affirmative action program and merely look for a program dealing with this topic. Now the difference among those who really understand that they are competing in a global market is readily evident as they refuse quick fixes, realize that significant problems require analytical solutions, and understand that a long-term view is needed to bring about meaningful results.

The use of a competency-based approach provides for integrated, flexible, and responsive training and facilitates lifelong learning, the new international trend. Organizations are identifying their competencies— what is the actual gap and the curriculum needed to conquer competitive advantage. New individual skills are a necessary condition for new organizational capabilities, but they are not sufficient to guarantee the development of such abilities. Organization-wide learning will require critical masses of individuals operating in new ways and will require new infrastructures that support learning.

The number of worldwide employees who receive training has increased steadily for years. The largest training budget amount is usually spent on managers, professionals, and sales personnel. At the same time, the transformation of companies from domestic to international organizations is leading to a whirlwind of ever-changing terminology, technology, and resources.

As they have expanded their markets, multinational corporations have brought with them into the emerging regions the concepts of total quality management (TQM), empowerment, team building, and delegating. Emphasis for several years now has been placed on developing corporate vision, reengineering, benchmarking, partnering, and outsourcing. Perhaps the most pervasive issue has been the restructuring of the workforce into teams.

This phenomenon has moved corporations to an emphasis on personal responsibility and improved performance—the push to deliver ever greater competence and productivity in the workplace. Partnering either *within the company* with other individuals, teams or departments or *outside the company* with suppliers/vendors, consultants or other entities through joint ventures is pervasive. Diversity training is increasing along with more emphasis on ethics and values. And as a result of the globalization of business, an increase in cross-cultural or global training is also occurring.

Professional skills and knowledge needed to manage modern business operations have not been developed either through the formal educational system or in industry. The need to obtain new competencies is so great, a combination of several solutions will be required including effective employment services, improved recruitment and staffing efforts, and retraining the existing workforce. Some evidence is appearing that organizations around the world are taking charge of this educational gap, not waiting for a government solution. Universities are initiating a more significant partnership with private companies. An increasing number of organizations are creating their own corporate universities in a clear demonstration of, and commitment to, life-long learning. New approaches to workforce education (either one-on-one and small groups) are needed to teach a wide range of job-related skills, while diagnosing specific learning needs and problems. Since the new economy stresses continuous learning, employees also will have to increase their ability to learn how to learn.

Focus on Performance

A strong focus of the multinational still remains on technical, job specific skill building. Performance is the key issue. No program, that professes to develop employee skills, is good unless the participants are able to use the skills in real life situations after the program.

Computer Based Training and Multimedia are gradually being introduced. An increased interest is seen in these programs, especially from those who include consistent learning concepts in their development and application. However, the development of these programs remains too expensive except for the largest and most profitable companies. Rapid change can be expected due to demands to accelerate competency curves while decreasing expenses and limiting overhead. On-line learning is expected to come from powerful interactive advisory systems. Performance technology and performance support will be one of the key development issues also.

Processes are often changing and key terms such as benchmarking, open learning, mentoring, improving on-the-job management performance, and self-paced learning materials are frequently discussed. Environmental Awareness Training is becoming a priority for some corporations. Coaching, 360° Feedback, Self-Assessment, and Assessment Centers are often added to corporate executive programs. Consultative Selling is also a clear trend. Information technology is increasingly used as sales support systems. As a natural influence, Performance Sales Teams are more common.

In addition, extremely sharp competition brought on by the opening of the European market, NAFTA, and other cooperating country agreements, and by worldwide technology changes has forced companies to realize that success, if not survival, requires an organizational ability to adapt and to be flexible. It also requires an unprecedented ability to think and act strategically.

Partnerships with local and international universities are a growing trend, and specific projects are a part of the training programs. Quality tools have become a common language and customer service is also a key issue. Team Management, Self-Directed Teams, and Team Performance are an integrated part of new organizational structure and architecture. Outdoor Training is often used as an approach to teamwork.

In the global marketplace, the goal of multinational corporations has shifted from bringing in expatriate managers to developing local managers who understand both the corporation's managerial style and the home culture. Computer technology is making it easier for middle managers and upper level managers to catch up—and often surpass—the managers from the multinational's host country in the new skills learning curve.

Individual Accountability

Emphasis is on accountability—understanding what it is and how it can be fostered among all employees, leaders, those in middle management and on the production floor. Leaders are no longer considered only responsible for company progress (the bottom line) but are responsible also for the personal development of their employees. Therefore, they need to develop mentoring and coaching skills.

A growing emphasis is placed on building international information networks so that employees can be part of, and take responsibility for, company development. Companies are also focusing on visible corporate strategies (not just something that top management is involved in), on productivity, and on what each employee contributes to the value adding activity of the company. Responsibility, accountability, and value-driven leadership are seen as the cornerstones of leadership for the future.

Responding to broader social trends, corporations will continue to focus on ethics. Work itself is being rethought, from being the drudgery of earning a paycheck to being the gratification that comes from meaningful work. Because of a need for balance, employees are looking for more meaning out of their work lives as well as their personal lives. Corporate CEOs will talk intently about corporate soul as there is growing evidence that value-driven companies outperform their competitors.

Customer Focus

The emphasis of the Industrial Age was on manufacturing and production. Today's company leaders are finding it difficult to move from a production mindset to a customer focus. Corporations that view themselves as producers think their technology creates products while customers believe their needs create products. With growing international competition, the customer is king, and loyal customers want their convenience to come first. They want customization, variety, and quality at an affordable cost.

Successful organizations know that constant innovation comes from listening to customers and empowering employees to make decisions on the spot. The skills of customer service specialists will be constantly upgraded as they continue to create more value for the customer.

With the current drive for quality, customer-focused and value-added service, all knowledge workers have to continuously improve their work processes so that effort to bring about change is in response to their customers' needs to obtain fast and better service and personalized attention.

Corporations are learning that customer service is not just a training course to be taught. A company that learns how to think like a customer must get to the specific product and customer level. Its products must be decentralized by product and industry type. Companies will also extend their product knowledge, technology, and training to customers and suppliers and partner with them for future success. Customers will become as big a learning market as company employees.

Customization

Human resource departments that have focused on creating an adaptive culture realize that prepackaged, one-size-fits-all solutions no longer work. They see each problem and opportunity and each individual as being unique, and they search for unique solutions. Their new competencies include a macro perspective on the new global marketplace, the ability to quickly assess people and systems, and leading edge organizational management knowledge and information. They have changed permanently and will continue to do so.

To a large extent, organizations have reinvented themselves, and employees are coming to terms with this paradigm. To maximize the potential of people in new organizations, the mandate of human resources management is to become a strategic player in a process of renewal.

The Application of Technology

In recent years, technological innovation has fostered considerable change in manufacturing processes. Significant automation and an increase in the use of computer-related technology have caused workers—who were once considered to have sufficient skills for lifetime employment—to learn new skills and processes to sustain their employment in an ever-changing environment. One-fourth to nearly half of manufacturing industries including industrial machines, fabricated metals, electronic instruments and equipment, and transportation equipment manufacturing—now use computer-aided design and computer-aided engineering in their overall operations. Many of the companies in these industries also use computer-controlled technology on the factory floor.

Trends in computing that will affect the use of technology and training are:
- Digital electronics
- Optical data storage
- Smaller, more powerful computers
- Networks with distributed computing such as Internet

While technological inventions will continue to proliferate, the applications of this technology into practical use for learning and performance will receive the highest priority.

The demands of international competition will continue to change the way businesses are organized and operated. Long distance communication and information networks will blur corporate and national boundaries even more than today.

Because of the emphasis on specialized information and expertise, teams of full-time employees, consultants, partners, and outsourced workers will be responsible for the design of key processes and projects. Improving performance in negotiation, decision making, and problem solving will be necessary for all team members.

Fluid structures will have to provide feedback for on-the-job development and continuous learning. Different appraisal tools will continue to be used. But must of all, the workforce will have to change a strong paradigm still in use—from *working harder* to *working smarter*. And this must be accelerated to *working smarter faster* as the global market demands competitiveness, flexibility, quickness, competency, quality, and high performance.

Management practices and training strategies can only be meaningful to the workforce when they are fully anchored in local roots to promote and increase workplace effectiveness.

Diversity and Cultural Differences

The main problem faced by trainers delivering programs in various countries has been the programs' lack of cultural sensitivity and the trainers' unfamiliarity with the environment in which they were working.

As increased globalization drives the diversity of the workforce, organizations must also increase their effort to help workers understand cultural differences. They must learn how to incorporate diverse values, ethics, and workstyles into their practices, products, and services.

When transferring programs from one country to another, a thorough analysis of many factors must be made to adapt the concepts and skill development to the local workers.

- A decision must be made on the training language. Many companies use bilingual training teams or interpreters. Using interpreters may be necessary but requires careful management, and experience indicates that the quality of interpretation varies greatly.
- The composition of the training group needs to be examined. Workers from some nations are accustomed to hierarchy and distance between employees at different levels in the organizational structure. In some instances, separate training programs should focus on different levels of staff since including people at too many different levels may not provide the best learning environment in certain countries.
- Course content, case studies, and examples should be based on an understanding of the culture and business environment. Trainers should not use examples which are not within the scope of experience for the participating workers.
- Cultural learning styles must be taken into account as well. Some cultures prefer concrete rather than abstract concepts; structured training programs are better for these cultures rather than programs which are loosely designed. In addition, more preparation and time should be allotted to non-technical training in such local cultures and should continue throughout the training initiative. Giving feedback, gathering and sharing information, identifying and solving problems, setting goals and achieving plans, and working as part of a team all fall into this category.
- Employees need to be told *why* they are learning—telling them what to do is not enough. So, many practices that are culturally bound need to be modified to work in different cultural settings. Training methods need to be modified due to different communication styles. For example, openly managing conflict works in American and some European cultures where communication is open and direct. In other countries, conflict is often managed indirectly to preserve face.
- In some regions, trainers and teachers are expected to lecture, and students are expected to be passive. So in these locales, *learning* is being able to explain what the teacher said. Active training methods and objectives can be successful in these regions but are different and need to be carefully explained. For example, action learning and

experiential activities can work but only if they are introduced by
explaining the objectives and key learning points. Do not expect explicit
feedback from trainees. Read the context and non-verbals.

- In many countries, materials cannot be borrowed from libraries or
purchased. Training materials are virtually unavailable, taking much
longer to accomplish tasks and gather resources than in the United States
and Europe. Being resourceful and scouting out resources locally and
internationally is a necessity.

The task ahead for human resource professionals is to revisit their own
cultural symbols and values instead of taking them as pre-defined or given
and use them to evaluate any imported materials so they reflect both global
and local perspectives. Hence HRD professionals have to recognize the
impact of cultural values on business behavior and how these values are
manifested in the workplace through managerial practices of leading,
communicating, motivating, planning, organizing, resolving conflict, and
negotiating.

Third World and Emerging Countries

Uniformity of performance needs and topics are also found in Third World
Countries. Many people are living for the first time in a new democratic
era, and the democratic process fosters commitment and responsibility to
shared goals. Learning democratic processes is as vital to a transition to a
more competitive organization and country as are individual and team
business skills. The entrepreneurial spirit is going to be intensified, with
the help of the information superhighways and high technology.
Organizations made up of autonomous teams with market-like freedoms
need effective processes for everyone to participate in shaping the bigger
picture. Empowerment will continue as a key issue. Also, the individualistic
approach will need to become more group oriented. Working with people
to reduce selfishness will be one of the biggest challenges and the only way
to change the environment.

Most national governments throughout the world are actively seeking
multinational corporations and making it attractive for them to come and
invest. They have also realized that developing—at the technical and
university level, as well as within the workforce—good skilled managers
is essential for building an infrastructure that will support a modern
technology-based global marketplace.

However, most training in Third World Countries is focused on building capabilities to make a successful transition to a free market economy. Privatization programs are a key factor for successful transition to a market economy.   Training is focused on economic restructuring, democracy building, and enhancing the quality of life, and funding has been designated for educational and training purposes.

The economic situation has resulted in the production-oriented management mindset carried over from the Industrial Revolution rather than the customer-oriented management viewpoint needed in the Information Age. Decades of an emphasis on producing quantity has made customer focus and product quality a secondary goal. Organizational structures in these areas tend to be hierarchical with power concentrated in a few managing directors. Management behavior is control-oriented and paternalistic. Information is especially controlled and is shared sparingly.

In general, organizational collaboration is not valued. As multinationals move into these regions, caution must be given to Western managers who attempt to practice Western management styles. It is unreasonable to expect employees who worked for managers under the previous system to change their attitudes and expectations about managers. Management practices, such as open communication and empowerment, are viewed by many old-style managers and employees with skepticism.

Significant gaps also exist between the workforce competencies required to move the regions into a competitive free market economy and the skills and knowledge of the existing workforce.

A Look at Tomorrow

Training classes as we know them today will not disappear—they will simply become one method of helping workers learn. We must make a significant leap in workplace learning within the next few years as we come to understand that learning involves more than absorbing information. It also includes creating new solutions to problems not yet fully defined.

Increasingly, corporate training will yield to individual learning. Workplace learning will be unavoidable, often chaotic, and constantly changing. The task of the global organization—its human resource professionals, its executives, its managers, and all employees—will be to continuously seek what is new and important, and to adapt it to the purpose and needs of its workers and customers. As Margaret Wheatley says in

"The Future of Workplace Learning and Performance" (*Training & Development*, May 1994), "Learning will be a description of how we live—the difference between our survival and our demise....There is no avoiding this future. But those who embrace it gracefully will find that learning has become their constant and predominant work."